Alive
in the Spirit

Written by

Rickey A. Andreas **Jonathan Lewis**
C. A. Brewer **Daniel L. Segraves**

This book is designed for personal or group study.

WORD AFLAME®
PUBLICATIONS

PENTECOSTAL PUBLISHING HOUSE
8855 DUNN ROAD
HAZELWOOD, MO 63042-2299

Word Aflame Elective Series

Alive in the Spirit

WHY? A Study of Christian Standards
Spiritual Growth and Maturity
Bible Doctrines: Foundation of the Church
Salvation: Key to Eternal Life
The Bible: Its Origin and Use
Strategy for Life for Singles and Young Adults
Spiritual Leadership/Successful Soulwinning
Your New Life
Friendship, Courtship, and Marriage
Purpose at Sunset
Values That Last
Meet the United Pentecostal Church International
Facing the Issues
The Holy Spirit
Life's Choices

Family Life Selections

The Christian Youth
The Christian Woman
The Christian Man
The Christian Parent

Editorial Staff

R. M. Davis . . . . .Edito

P. D. Buford . . . . Associate Edito

J. L. Hall . . . . .Editor in Chi
United Pentecostal Church International

CURRICULUM COMMITTEE: James E. Boatman, P. D. Buford, Dan Butle
R. M. Davis, J. L. Hall, G. W. Hassebrock, Garth E. Hatheway, E. E. Jolle
Chester L. Mitchell, Ronald Nation, W. C. Parkey, David L. Reynold
Charles A. Rutter, R. L. Wyser.

Foreword

Daniel L. Segraves
Executive Vice-President and
Chairman of the Department
of Theology
Christian Life College
Stockton, California

There is no better description of first-century Christian life than "life in the Spirit."

Jesus indicated that it is by means of the Holy Spirit that we are introduced to the kingdom of God (John 3:5). He further declared that those who believe in Him would receive the Holy Spirit, which would continuously flow forth through them as a living river (John 7:37-39).

The birthday of the church was characterized by the rushing of the Holy Spirit into the room where the disciples waited. Each was filled with the Holy Spirit. (See Acts 2:1-4.) Peter, the first spokesman of the assembled believers, proclaimed that the gift of the Holy Spirit was for all who would be called by the Lord God (Acts 2:38-39). Throughout the Book of Acts, the Holy Spirit came upon those who believed. (See Acts 8:17; 9:17; 10:44-45; 15:8; 19:6.)

So the Christian life begins with the Holy Spirit. (See Galatians 3:3). But that is not the end of the story. Christian growth and maturity is also a matter of being led by the Spirit. Being led by the Spirit of God characterizes a person as a son of God (Romans 8:14). To some degree, it is possible to determine how successfully we are being led by the Spirit by the evidence of the Spirit's fruit in our lives (Galatians 5:22-25). Indeed, to be filled with the

Holy Spirit is not just a one-time experience. Paul urged the Ephesians to be continuously filled with the Spirit (Ephesians 5:18).

In addition to initiation into the Christian life and growth as a Christian, there is also a third dimension of life in the Spirit. That is the realm of supernatural ministry made possible by the gifts of the Spirit (I Corinthians 12-14). Spiritual giftedness cannot be equated with spiritual maturity, but the role of the Holy Spirit at work through His people in miracles, signs, and wonders is central to the New Testament. (See Acts 2:22, 43; 4:29-31; 5:12; 6:8; 8:6-8; 14:3; Romans 15:18-19; Hebrews 2:3-4.)

Those of us who gladly claim the first-century experience of Christian initiation by the Holy Spirit should also embrace the full range of experiences shared by our early brothers and sisters. This includes Spirit-directed growth and ministry.

With the passing of the years, I have become ever more convinced that a primary factor distinguishing the New Covenant from the Old Covenant is the continuing rich presence of the Holy Spirit in, through, and around believers, ushering them into the kingdom of God, sustaining and nurturing them as they enjoy life in that kingdom, and equipping them to minister powerfully and effectively to those who are hurting.

Contents

Living in the Spirit

For to be carnally minded is death; but to be spiritually minded is life and peace.

Romans 8:6

Start with the Scriptures

Romans 8:1-9
Galatians 6:1
I Peter 2:5

It is still real! Abundant life is still available.

Often the Scriptures speak of the Holy Spirit as refreshing waters. The Spirit is like a river of life flowing out to redeem and bless mankind. No matter how they are described (whether proceeding from a smitten rock in the wilderness or from a glorious throne in heaven), these waters of blessing are from God.

The river of God is bountiful. In Genesis 2:10 the writer saw that the river "was parted, and became into four heads." Its abundance, then and now, refreshes the soul of an individual who thirsts for God. Moreover, it is available to all: "And let him that is athirst come. And whosoever will, let him take of the water of life freely" (Revelation 22:17).

Why would anyone stand on the banks of a mighty river with a tin cup when there are "waters to swim in, a river that could not be passed over" (Ezekiel 47:5)? Why stand on the shoreline when just beyond are the depths of God's love?

Because of the Need

The greatest thing ever accomplished for mankind was done because God saw our need. Oh, how dire the need! We were "dead in trespasses and sins" (Ephesians 2:1) and "walked according to the course of this world, according to the prince of the power of the air" (Ephesians 2:2). Hopelessly and helplessly we struggled in sin.

Man's greatest need brought about the Incarnation—God revealed in Jesus. Empowered by the Spirit of God, Jesus led men into a living relationship with the heavenly Father. He prepared His disciples to receive the Holy Ghost at Pentecost, but the Pentecostal experience was not just a phenomenon of the first century. This is an experience where today a believer can enter the presence of God—not into the Holy of Holies but into Jesus Christ. It is Christ living in us and our living in Christ.

What, really, is "living in the Spirit"? It is abiding in Jesus Christ (John 15:4-7, 10). It means living in God, living in the flow of His love, and being prompted and motivated by the force of His presence. It means being cleansed and sanctified, being continually cared for and yet constantly set free. Liberty to live above sin comes only through the Spirit of God. The apostle Paul stated, "For in him

8

we live, and move, and have our being" (Acts 17:28).

Spiritual life by the Holy Spirit is available to all people. Jesus clearly demonstrated this by His visit to the people in Samaria, who were despised by the Jews. Jesus admonished the Samaritan woman at the well, "If thou knewest the gift of God, and who it is that saith to thee, Give me to drink; thou wouldest have asked of him, and he would have given thee living water" (John 4:10). She was a Samaritan, a stranger to the covenant of Israel, but Jesus offered to open a fountain of life to the woman. Leaving her waterpot behind, she hurried to tell others of the One who knew all things.

Jesus knows that our greatest thirst will never be satisfied with worldy achievements. Fame and fortune will never meet this need. The greatest thirst of man can be satisfied only by the presence of God Himself.

Luke chapter 10 gives an account of three men who saw a man stripped, wounded, and left for dead. The priest may have viewed the wounded man as a ceremonial contamination; the Levite may have seen him as a dangerous inconvenience; but the Samaritan saw the wounded man as a fellow human in need.

It cost the Samaritan a good deal to meet the need. But, then, it cost the priest and the Levite dearly not to respond. Something dies within the individual who fails to have compassion for others.

There is no physical description given of the Samaritan, but in his actions—in coming to where the injured man lay, in binding up his wounds, in paying a price for his restoration—the resemblance to Jesus Christ is unmistakable. We never resemble Jesus Christ any stronger than when we meet a need in the life of a hopeless person in despair.

Drawn by the Spirit

God responded to the greatest need of mankind. How overwhelming His response was—Jesus Christ born at Bethlehem! It was mercy shining through the dark clouds of judgment and death. It was the garment of love covering the nakedness of man's sin. By mercy and love God would draw all mankind to repentance.

It is all right for the sinner to weep at an altar of repentance—weep profoundly, weep profusely. God is not offended at the sinner's honesty. It is God's Spirit that draws him. God knows the depth of the sinner's need, and He wishes to plunge him into the depth of His love. "You will not weep long in repentance," someone has said, "until your sorrow will be turned into joy." (See Psalm 30:5.) "The sacrifices of God are a broken spirit: a broken and a contrite heart, O God, thou wilt not despise" (Psalm 51:17).

The Spirit always draws people in one direction—toward Jesus Christ. (See John 16:13.) People sense this when they hear anointed preaching. Just as the Word of God exalts Jesus Christ, the unction of the Holy Ghost will do the same.

The Spirit will draw us to prayer. In some nations, five times each day a muezzin makes a public call for Muslims to stop for prayer, but it is the Holy Spirit from within us who calls Christians to prayer. While the Muslim drops to his knees and faces Mecca, the Christian prays and looks toward Christ.

Jude 20 speaks of "praying in the Holy Ghost." If we pray in the Spirit, we will pray with conviction. We push aside the desires of our flesh. This does not necessarily mean we are unconscious of our surroundings. Rather, it means that we are more conscious of heavenly things.

A pastor once said that it takes time to pray all the cares of life out of our thinking. Our minds are often cluttered by pressures and problems. Perhaps that is why some Christians faint in a time of trouble. "But," wrote Isaiah, "they that wait upon the LORD shall renew their strength; they shall mount up with wings as eagles; they shall run, and not be weary; and they shall walk, and not faint" (Isaiah 40:31).

We shall walk in the Spirit if we attend to the things of the Spirit. The choice is ours. We can choose to live superficially or spiritually. The low road is dismal and dangerous; the high road leads us to a fresh faith and a renewed vision of Jesus Christ.

Our interests will change dramatically if we choose to live in the Spirit. No longer will our excitement come from following the careers of sports stars. The celebrities of television will lose their appeal. Much of what the world calls thrilling will seem dull and mundane. Christ, for us, will become supremely important—overwhelmingly more important than anything else!

We can choose to live a spiritual life in Jesus Christ. We can read our Bibles enthusiastically; we can pray fervently; we can worship wholeheartedly. Church attendance can become exciting, and so can giving ourselves and our finances to the cause of God. Our choices can be correct choices. Despite the certain challenges, and despite the occasional failures, we can be overcomers through Christ. The choice is ours to make.

The Finest of Fruit

"And on the banks of the river on both its sides, there shall grow all kinds of trees for food; their leaf shall not fade, nor shall their fruit fail [to meet the demand]" (Ezekiel 47:12, *The Amplified Bible*).

It takes time to develop spirituality. There is no sudden harvest by which a believer becomes mature overnight. A day-by-day walk with God is involved.

Once we have been born again we must still "learn" Christ. (See Ephesians 4:20.) That is, as we fellowship with the Lord we will learn of His will and way.

One of the surest signs that a person is developing spiritually is that he manifests the love of Christ. "The love of God is shed abroad in our hearts by the Holy Ghost which is given unto us" (Romans 5:5). This is the Spirit's progressive work. The selfishness and rebellion of the fleshly nature can be overcome only by dependence on the Holy Ghost. Love is the very nature of God (I John 4:8). When we allow hatred and malice to develop within our hearts, we push aside the spiritual nature and succumb to our fleshly desires. (See I John 3:14.) When we forgive others and are reconciled to them, we please God.

Years ago two Christian men disagreed as to where to pile the wood for a church stove. One man became adamant, then angered. He finally left for home. His attitude was so bitter that he never attended the church again.

Such are the works or practices of the flesh, but the work which God's Spirit accomplishes within a believer is far different. "The fruit of the Spirit is love, joy, peace, longsuffering, gentleness, goodness, faith, meekness, temperance: against such there is no law. And they that are Christ's have crucified the flesh with the affections and lusts" (Galatians 5:22-24). In the following verse Paul exhorted, "If we live in the Spirit, let us also walk in the Spirit" (Galatians 5:25).

The fruit of the Spirit is evidence of the new life within the believer and also of the death of his old ways. "Except a corn of wheat fall into the ground and die, it abideth alone: but if it die, it bringeth forth much fruit" (John 12:24). The fruit of the Spirit is the product of living in harmony with God and of denying the flesh. Our own nature fails to produce this love, joy, and peace. The production of such precious fruit is beyond the highest of human capabilities, "for it is God which worketh in you both to will and to do of his good pleasure" (Philippians 2:13).

Shortcuts and Substitutes

There are no shortcuts when it comes to living spiritually. It is not necessarily an easy path. Complete dedication to Jesus Christ and devotion to God's Word are necessary for a person to walk in the Spirit. Living a separated lifestyle is essential—a life separated from worldy pleasures and set apart unto the Lord for His will and pleasure.

Many, unfortunately, try to take an easier route. They are content to splash in the stagnant pools along the shore. They may create some waves in their little ponds, but because these people have a poor understanding of Jesus Christ, they lack depth and discernment. In their walk with God, such individuals are easily distracted and easily discouraged. They place too little value on obedience to the Word of God. They actually may become "the enemies of the cross of Christ" (Philippians 3:18) because they "mind earthly things" (Philippians 3:19).

One man stated, "I would travel for thousands of miles to see a miracle." He was not content with sound, biblical teaching. This individual wanted to see the sensational. He seemed unaware that Christians are never instructed to follow signs. (The devil can, and does, produce signs.) Jesus promised as He gave the great commission, "These signs shall follow them that believe; In my name shall they cast out devils; they shall speak with new tongues; they shall take up serpents; and if they drink any deadly thing, it shall not hurt them; they shall lay hands on the sick, and they shall recover" (Mark 16:17-18). God intends for the signs to follow the believer, not for the believer to follow the signs.

The gifts of the Spirit are like power tools. Unfortunately, although the gifts are available to all who have received the Holy Ghost, not everyone is mature enough to use them wisely (I Corinthians 12, 13).

A young Christian once prayed earnestly to be used in the gifts of the Spirit. He related afterward that the Lord spoke to his heart and said, "You first need the fruit of the Spirit." Wisely, he received the admonition, and later God used him as he had requested.

Perhaps it is in the area of humility that most believers need to exercise caution. Spiritual gifts are not a measure of one's spirituality. God gives the gifts to edify, or build up, the church as a whole—never for self-glorification. The individual whom Christ chooses to use in a gift has learned to yield to the promptings of the Spirit, at least in one area. He has simply become a conduit of a particular type of blessing. As wonderful as this is, the individual still needs instruction. In fact, his willingness to receive teaching under godly leadership is a greater proof of his spirituality than his being used in the gifts. (See I Corinthians 3:1-2; Hebrews 5:12.)

The Eddy

An eddy is a current of water moving against the main stream. It is a back-circling flow of water that sometimes forms a whirlpool.

Whirlpools may have a strong vortical motion, or they may be suctionless. Even the suctionless whirlpools may be dangerous, however, for they can becalm a small ship or sweep it against rugged rocks.

A believer may sometimes feel that crosscurrents are hindering his progress. Struggle as he will, a strong eddy flows against his best intentions. He feels becalmed, or worse still, driven.

We can expect that there will be eddies and even whirlpools in our lives. We should expect opposition

14

and disappointment. We will, at times, face a struggle just to maintain our spiritual course. According to Ephesians 6:12, our opponents are supernatural rather than physical.

Temptations, like eddies, can be dangerous obstructions. They can bring confusion to our minds and fear to our hearts.

Struggle and victory is the way of the spiritual life. We have launched out into the things of God, but there is a fleshly nature that would pull us back. We have begun to yield ourselves to the Spirit, but the carnal mind suggests we should serve the desires of the flesh. At stake is our eternal destiny. "For to be carnally minded is death; but to be spiritually minded is life and peace" (Romans 8:6).

The more we submit to God the more victory we enjoy and the more we resist the devil. (See James 4:7.) We are to yield control of our thoughts, as well as our actions, to the Lord. We have actually begun to share the thoughts and attitudes of Christ Himself. (See I Corinthians 2:16; Philippians 2:5.)

We can have victory over temptation, even as Job rejected his wife's counsel to curse God, as Joseph resisted the allurements of Potiphar's wife, and as Daniel refused to defile himself with the king's meat and wine. Our struggles may be difficult, and they may be protracted. But Christ has promised never to leave us or forsake us, and through Him we can be conquerors. "For in that he himself hath suffered being tempted, he is able to succour them that are tempted" (Hebrews 2:18).

Where Rivers Flow

The Scriptures are plain as to the blessing God would like to pour out upon us. David declared of the Lord, "Thou visitest the earth, and waterest it: thou greatly enrichest it with the river of God, which is full of water: thou preparest them corn, when thou hast so provided for it" (Psalm 65:9). Again, in Psalm 36:8, David wrote that the children of men "shall be abundantly satisfied with the fatness of thy house; and thou shalt make them drink of the river of thy pleasures."

"Where," one might ask, "does God's river flow?" Since Proverbs 21:1 declares, "He turneth it whithersoever he will," what course does God's mighty stream follow?

God chooses the lowlands of life's experiences to be the places where people will benefit the most. He chooses the valleys below the mountain ridges. He chooses the lower glens instead of the higher heights. It is not in the hills that the rivers flow the deepest or the widest. Instead the rivers spread their richness throughout the bottomlands.

"All the rivers run into the sea" (Ecclesiastes 1:7). The Lord's ultimate goal is mankind's utmost good. In the Scriptures the sea is sometimes a type of restless and rebellious humanity (Isaiah 57:20; Revelation 13:1). But even when man is tossed to and fro by sin, the Lord wishes to pour in the freshness of His Spirit.

Living in the Spirit is the highest of privileges. There is life and hope in the river of God's presence. There is peace, there is joy. The waters of this river produce a tree whose leaves are "for the healing of the nations" (Revelation 22:2).

The believer who continually delights in the ways of the Lord shall himself be as a flourishing plant. "He shall be like a tree planted by the rivers of water, that bringeth forth his fruit in his season" (Psalm 1:3).

Test Your Knowledge

What aspect of the Spirit's work is presented by each of the following verses of Scripture? The first one is done for you.

1. "Howbeit when he, the Spirit of truth, is come, he will guide you into all truth" (John 16:13). Guidance

2. "It is the Spirit that quickeneth" (John 6:63).

_____

3. "He that abideth in me, and I in him, the same bringeth forth much fruit" (John 15:5). _____

4. "The Spirit itself maketh intercession for us with groanings which cannot be uttered" (Romans 8:26). _____

5. "The love of God is shed abroad in our hearts by the Holy Ghost which is given unto us" (Romans 5:5). _____

6. "The Spirit itself beareth witness with our spirit, that we are the children of God" (Romans 8:16).

_____

Apply Your Knowledge

The Holy Ghost is a gift, but we ourselves must decide how we will maintain this precious possession.

Consider your choices. Ask yourself some personal questions such as: "Do the things that I listen to and the literature that I read need to be changed?" "Are my words encouraging to other Christians?" "Are my thoughts wholesome and clean?" "Do I worship God with my whole heart?"

Expand Your Knowledge

Ephesians 2:2 and 4:17-19 speak of the walk of the past (walking as a sinner). There are at least five other references in this same epistle which deal with the new walk (walking as a Christian). Find these references and apply them to your personal experiences as a Christian.

2 Spiritual Discipline

Howbeit this kind goeth not out but by prayer and fasting.

Matthew 17:21

There is no way to exhaust the subject of spiritual disciplines in this chapter. Perhaps, though, we can effectively address prayer and fasting, two important spiritual disciplines.

Prayer

It seems that one of the most difficult spiritual disciplines to consistently maintain in the lives of God's people is that of prayer. The reason is clear. The enemy of our soul does not want us to pray. However, Jesus gave specific and clear instructions for the church to pray: "And he spake a parable unto them to this end, that men ought always to pray, and not to faint" (Luke 18:1). Paul the apostle emphasized prayer's importance in I Thessalonians 5:17: "Pray without ceasing." Prayer is necessary for Christians, for it is their communication with God. By our talking to God and God talking to us in prayer, we have the direction and guidance we need in life.

The Wisdom and Virtue to Pray

The wisdom of God teaches us to pray, but the virtue to pray (that is the desire to put all else aside and pray) must come from our own heart. Prayer is not difficult, however. When a person presses through the fear and confusion and learns to enjoy prayer, praying becomes easy.

Paul stated, "Let every man be fully persuaded in his own mind" (Romans 14:5). The psalmist said, "As for me, I will call upon God; and the LORD shall save me. Evening, and morning, and at noon, will I pray, and cry aloud: and he shall hear my voice" (Psalm 55:16-17). To pray involves a mental commitment. One must choose to pray. If there is any discipline of our lives that we should diligently develop, it is the discipline of prayer.

The Skill of Prayer

It is easy to fulfill that which we know to do when we have the skill to do it. In regard to the skill of prayer, there is beneficial information in the *My Father's House* new converts course. In this course (available from the General Home Missions Division), two absolutes are mentioned for successful praying.

The first absolute is systematic prayer. We must organize our time to pray or have a specific time to pray. We must be specific in our requests of God. The prophet Isaiah stated, "Produce your cause, saith the LORD; bring forth your strong reasons, saith the King of Jacob" (Isaiah 41:21). How do we want God to bless? How do we praise Him? Is our prayer specific?

The second absolute is complete prayer. This involves method. With a method, we discipline the mind and do not allow it to wander.

For an example of method, consider the prayer wheel found in *My Father's House* new converts course. It offers twelve sections of a complete prayer time: praise, forgiveness, confession, petition, intercession, Bible reading, meditation, thanksgiving, praying the Word, singing, listening, and praise.

This schedule will help remove any fear or dread of prayer. Of course, this is not to suggest that one has not prayed until he has prayed all twelve steps of the prayer schedule.

In addition to the prayer wheel, we should always:

1. Pray in Jesus' name. This allows one to pray according to God's unlimited power;

2. Pray within God's Word or within His will (James 4:3; I John 5:14);

3. Pray according to God's nature. God is holy and just, giving only that which is according to His nature;

4. Shut some doors. Shut the door to iniquity (Psalm 66:18); shut the door to evil (I Peter 3:12); shut the door to selfishness (Isaiah 58:9-10); shut the door to unbelief and fear.

Thanksgiving in Prayer

There is an old proverb that says, "One thing at a time." Sometimes, however, two things at a time are better, especially when the two are prayer and thanksgiving. Prayer coupled with thanksgiving and praise can be likened to the two cherubim on the ark of the covenant that must not be separated.

In the model prayer that Jesus gave, He said, "Our Father which art in heaven, Hallowed be thy name" (Luke 11:2). The relationship mentioned there is that of a son to the Father. We were sinners but have been saved by grace and have been made the sons of God. Therefore we acknowledge Him as our heavenly Father. We praise Him for His mighty acts and worship Him for who He is, giving glory to His name.

David, who is a great tutor of worship and prayer, was careful to mingle prayer with praise. For example, Psalm 51, written after his sin with Bathsheba, was probably filled with groans and tears. He began, "Have mercy upon me, O God, according to thy lovingkindness: according unto the multitude of thy tender mercies blot out my transgressions" (Psalm 51:1). But he concluded, "O LORD, open thou my lips; and my mouth shall shew forth thy praise" (Psalm 51:15).

It always seems that David warms himself into praise with the fire of prayer. Another example is found in Psalm 18:3. David said, "I will call upon the LORD, who is worthy to be praised: so shall I be saved from mine enemies."

Prayer with thanksgiving is infallibly effectual, giving the psalmist confidence: "So shall I be saved from mine enemies" (Psalm 18:3).

If combining thanksgiving with prayer is found in the Old Testament, how much more should we find it exhibited in the New Testament? Paul stated, "First, I thank my God through Jesus Christ for you all, that your faith is spoken of throughout the whole world. For God is my witness, whom I serve with my spirit in the gospel of his Son, that without ceasing I make mention of you always in my prayers" (Romans 1:8-9). We observe both thanksgiving and prayer.

Paul wrote in Philippians 1:3-4, "I thank my God upon every remembrance of you, Always in every prayer of mine for you all making request with joy."

In the Book of Acts there is a historical account of Paul and Silas in jail in stocks and bonds. The Bible records that in this time of distress Paul and Silas began to pray with thanksgiving: "And at midnight Paul and Silas prayed, and sang praises unto God: and the prisoners heard them" (Acts 16:25). The result of praying with thanksgiving brought liberty and freedom to them!

There are several reasons why we should mingle thanksgiving with prayer.

First of all, thanksgiving is the right spirit in which to come to God. The psalmist admonished, "Bless the LORD, O my soul, and forget not all his benefits" (Psalm 103:2). We as finite creatures can have an audience with the infinite Creator. The mercy seat of Calvary is available for us. He stands ready as the High Priest to bring reconciliation to lost mankind. One can boldly approach the throne of grace without fear or doubt when thanksgiving is blended with prayer. It is the right spirit in which to approach God.

Another reason we pray with thanksgiving is that while we remember His past goodness to us, we receive faith for the present. Prayer in faith can send us away full of the blessing of God. Jesus said, "All things, whatsoever ye shall ask in prayer, believing, ye shall receive" (Matthew 21:22).

Prayer without thanksgiving is selfish and lacks faith. Moreover, prayer without thanksgiving refuses submission of our will to God's will. Praying with thanksgiving destroys the leaven of self-will. Such praying places us in harmony with God's will so that our desires become like His desires. Jesus said, "If ye abide in me, and my words abide in you, ye shall ask what ye will, and it shall be done unto you" (John 15:7).

The results of praying with thanksgiving are many. *First, it brings the product of peace. Second, thanksgiving enables the soul to pray.* If there are times that one cannot seem to pray or that his prayer seems cold and formal, then he can begin to praise the Lord. Praising can dissolve the hard heart and allow prayer to flow like a river. *Third, thanksgiving opens the avenue of God's blessing.* (See II Chronicles 20:20-22.)

Finally, thanksgiving brings an end to waiting. We often must wait for answers to our prayers, but praise can bring us to the time where God can indulge us our requests.

One man said to a minister, "You say that we should always pray, but I've been praying for months and do not feel the peace of mind I need. In fact, I have more doubt."

The minister replied, "That is the result of selfish praying." So they went to prayer together and he admonished the man to glorify God. His waiting came to an end. When you begin to give thanks to God, the answer is on the way.

One song said it this way:
Oh yes, the answer's on the way, this I know.
Jesus said it, I believe it, and it's so.
Our heavenly Father knows the need before we pray.
You can rest assured the answer's on the way.

Understanding by Prayer

Understanding what one is trying to accomplish in prayer is very important. Prayer without understanding is difficult. *The secret of understanding is found in the matter of guidance and obedience.* Divine guidance requires an obedient response, which results in understanding.

The prophet Micah spoke to a rebellious and carnal people saying, "They know not the thoughts of the LORD, neither understand they his counsel" (Micah 4:12). One who may not perceive God or God's will usually prays without understanding. It is the knowledge of God—God's will and obedience to Him—that brings one to understanding and success in prayer.

One man said, "In my college days, I spent a great deal of time looking for the used textbook that had the answers written in to the exercises. The reason was just simply to have the answers." Simply knowing the answers is not sufficient. When one follows the guidance of the teacher's instruction, it is not necessary to know just the answer because he knows the way to arrive at the answer.

In the prayer that Jesus gave, He prayed, "Thine is the kingdom . . ." (Matthew 6:13). If a person can pray "thine is the kingdom," his praying will result in a life controlled by the will of God.

A person may ask, "How can I do the will of God unless I know what that will is?" Jesus set the precondition saying, "If any man will do his will, he shall know . . ." (John 7:17). We often want God to show us His plan and then decide. God wants us to be willing and then He enlightens. His enlightenment, guidance, and our obedience bring understanding.

Serving in Prayer

The Bible speaks of Anna, a prophetess, who "served God with fastings and prayers night and day" (Luke 2:37). We should understand that praying is a ministry. Like other ministries, there are challenges to overcome in the ministry of prayer.

Some of the common challenges are

• Shallow praying (without a true season of prayer);

• Fear of unfavorable answers;

• Praying aloud;

• Hindrances such as sin, wrong motives, idols in our lives, an unforgiving spirit, unbelief, a lack of generosity (Matthew 7:2), or emotions;

• Laziness;

• The mystery of prayer.

There is much to gain through prayer:

• The kingdom of God comes (Luke 11:1-2);

• Laborers are sent into the harvest (Matthew 9:37-38);

• Sinners are saved (I Timothy 2:1, 4);

• Backsliders are reclaimed (I John 5:16);

• Restoration occurs (Isaiah 62:6-7).

We know that victory, revival, success, and the kingdom of God are not for sale; they are beyond purchase. But regular, consistent prayer in our lives is a means of service to God whereby we can focus on the things that are important to God. We are empowered to focus on evangelizing the lost so that souls are born into the kingdom of God.

Agreement in Prayer

Some of the greatest spiritual and human battles are fought in the arena of prayer. Jesus said, "Verily I say unto you, Whatsoever ye shall bind on earth shall be bound in heaven: and whatsoever ye shall loose on earth shall be loosed in heaven. Again I say unto you, That if two of you shall agree on earth as touching any thing that they shall ask, it shall be done for them of my Father which is in heaven" (Matthew 18:18-19).

The context of Matthew 18 demonstrates the

authority of the church to "bind or loose" according to standards recognized in heaven. Though the passage of Scripture does not deal with personal prayer but church discipline, the principle of agreement is noteworthy.

In prayer, agreement should come prior to the request. This is illustrated in the instruction of Jesus regarding disciplinary action. (See Matthew 18:19.) When Christians observe this in principle, their prayers will reflect the will of God. Unity in the Spirit is imperative for successful praying. The key is being in "one accord" (agreement) with God. Prayer is hindered when a person is out of agreement with God, God's church, or fellow Christians.

Fasting

Fasting intensifies prayer. When they are linked together, a new relationship develops between the individual and Jesus Christ.

In our relationship with Jesus Christ, a right spirit is a humble spirit. Fasting is one way to humble ourselves before God. David said, "I humbled my soul with fasting" (Psalm 35:13). Though many perhaps would do away with fasting, Jesus modeled it and expects it. (See Matthew chapters 4 and 6.)

Isaiah 58

The nature of an acceptable fast is given in Isaiah 58. As in prayer, fasting should be done with the right motives and purpose:
- To loose the bands of wickedness;
- To undo the heavy burdens;
- To let the oppressed go free;
- To break every yoke;
- To deal bread to the hungry;
- To bring the poor that are cast out to our house;

- To cover the naked;
- To consider needs of family.

Obviously, God's purpose in our fasting is to humble ourselves, care about others, and search our hearts. That which cannot be seen when one is gratifying the flesh becomes perceptible during a fast.

Fasting according to the method mentioned in Isaiah 58:6-7 brings blessings.

- Light shall break forth as the morning;
- Health shall spring forth speedily;
- Righteousness shall go before us;
- The glory of the Lord shall be our rear guard;
- The Lord shall answer our call;
- The Lord shall say to our cry, "Here I am."

Food or Fasting

Jesus told His followers, "If any man will come after me, let him deny himself, and take up his cross daily, and follow me. For whosoever will save his life shall lose it: but whosoever will lose his life for my sake, the same shall save it" (Luke 9:23-24). The words of Jesus help us to understand the benefits of a disciplined life versus the consequences of an undisciplined life.

Food is necessary and we should enjoy it. However, anything that becomes more important to us than God becomes our idol—even food. Just as a person should organize his time to include prayer, he should also include a special time for fasting. This is discipline.

Obviously, this raises the question about the different types of fasting. A study of various people in Scripture reveals various types of fasting.

- Moses (Exodus 34:28);
- Elijah (I Kings 19:8);
- Ezra (Ezra 8:21-23);
- Nehemiah (Nehemiah 9:1);
- Esther (Esther 4);
- Daniel (Daniel 1:10-20);

- Nineveh (Jonah 3:5-10);
- Jesus (Matthew 4).

In each of these, one can see the various kinds and lengths of fasting. The three general types of fasting may be classified as (1) normal (Matthew 4:2); (2) partial (Daniel 10:3); and (3) absolute (Acts 9:9). Whichever is chosen, when we humble ourselves and discipline ourselves to fast, God will bring inspiration and power in our walk with Him.

God's Response to Prayer and Fasting

God delights in doing good things for those who pray and fast. He would not withhold any good thing. God responds!

In our prayer and fasting, we should through our disciplined life seek to glorify God. Paul said, "Whatsoever ye do, do all to the glory of God" (I Corinthians 10:31).

If we will continue praying and fasting, our self-will (flesh), will be submitted to God, and the glory of God will be revealed. God loves a humble, broken, and contrite spirit (Psalm 34:18). He is touched by those who cry out to Him (Psalm 9:12; 34:15).

While Martha busied herself with the natural things, Mary sat at the feet of Jesus. Jesus said, "Mary hath chosen that good part, which shall not be taken away from her" (Luke 10:42). We should withdraw from the things of the natural and consume the things of the spiritual. We have the opportunity to choose the good part of living for God—prayer and fasting.

Test Your Knowledge

1. What are two aspects of prayer?
2. What two absolutes are helpful for successful praying?

3. God will answer your prayer regardless of how you pray. (true or false)

4. Name five hindrances to prayer.

5. Guidance and obedience in prayer bring understanding. (true or false)

6. That which cannot be seen when one is gratifying the flesh becomes perceptible during a fast. (true or false)

7. Name three general types of fasting.

8. Spiritual discipline helps bring glory to God that He can reveal to us. (true or false)

Apply Your Knowledge

The best example of discipline is the life of Jesus Christ. It was prayer that impressed the disciples. They never asked Him to teach them to do miracles, but they did ask Him to teach them to pray. Never should prayer or fasting become a casualty in our lives. They should be a priority.

If we will humble ourselves, fast, and pray, God will reveal His glory. "The effectual fervent prayer of a righteous man availeth much" (James 5:16). Is this the pattern of the early church? Count the prayers and the miracles recorded in the Book of Acts, and you will discover the pattern for today's church.

Expand Your Knowledge

Many great books and publications have been authored by many Pentecostal authors. The Pentecostal Publishing House has many resources for this area of your life. However, the best book is your Bible. Link God's Word with prayer and fasting, and He will give you knowledge.

3 Living the Word of God

For ever, O Lord, thy word is settled in heaven.
Psalm 119:89

Start with the Scriptures

Psalm 119:97-109
II Timothy 3:16
II Peter 1:20-21

By definition, to "live the Word of God" is to "live in the Spirit," for the words of God are not just ink on paper; they are spirit, and they are life. (See John 6:63.) It is, of course, necessary to rightly divide "the word of truth" (II Timothy 2:15), or to correctly interpret it and apply it, in order for the Word to bring life. (See II Peter 3:16.)

How God Has Revealed Himself

For the first 2,500 years of human history, there was no written revelation from God. But this does not mean that no revelation of God existed during this time.

Even before He gave Moses the first written revelation, God communicated knowledge about Himself by means of His creation. This is usually called "general revelation." David described how creation communicated knowlege about God. (See Psalm 19:1-4.)

It may seem that this revelation of God is so impersonal as to be of little real value, but Paul declared that the testimony of creation reveals so much about God that those who reject it are "without excuse." (See Romans 1:18-21.) A simple observation of the created universe informs any thinking person that there is a God. These Gentiles had a level of knowledge of God ("they knew God"), but they rejected it in favor of religion of their own making.

Another aspect of general revelation is the knowledge of right and wrong communicated by the human conscience. (See Romans 2:14-15.) Paul did not mean to say that Gentiles will be saved merely by doing the best they know how to do. He used the example of the conscience to show that all men have a knowledge of right and wrong they do not necessarily live up to. This is clear in that the conscience both accuses and excuses. When it is violated, it accuses; when it is obeyed, it excuses.

Scripture, known as "special revelation" because it was given to the nation of Israel as opposed to the world at large (Romans 3:1-2), had its origin about 1,500 years before the time of Christ. The Bible claims to be an inerrant revelation of God that must be obeyed.

A Unique Revelation

There is no other book in the world like the Bible. Indeed, the world could not produce such a book. Even in our generation of high technology and computerization, the production of such a faultless book, on any subject, would be impossible. If we asked forty different men living today to each write a book on a common topic that would then be compiled into one book, the result would be a hopeless hodgepodge of ideas, philosophies, and viewpoints, even if all the writers knew each other and wrote at the same time. But the Holy Bible was written by some forty men, many of whom did not know each other, over a period of some 1,600 years! These men came from all kinds of backgrounds: kings, shepherds, farmers, lawyers, tax-collectors, physicians, fishermen. Yet, under the inspiration of God, they produced one glorious whole, without any contradiction.

The Effect of the Revelation

Wherever a society respects, reads, and lives by the Bible, it is lifted to new heights of character and morality. The Bible has a positive effect on the quality of life. Families are strengthened, and evil and wickedness are minimized in areas where the Word of God is honored. On the other hand, the quality of life sinks low where the Bible is not honored.

Confirmation of the Revelation

At one time, some scholars scoffed at historical records found in the Bible. They assumed the Bible was simply a book of myths because they had never found evidence that certain kings mentioned in the Bible had ever lived, or that certain cities had ever existed. But while it would be a mistake to say that the purpose of archaeology is to confirm the historical accounts in the Scripture, every archaeological discovery with any bearing on biblical statements has confirmed the accuracy of the Bible. Not once has the Bible been proven wrong in its accounts of history.

The Fulfillment of the Revelation

The Bible contains at least 6,000 specific prophecies. Thousands of them have already been fulfilled, precisely as given. Many prophecies had to do with the future of cities and kingdoms. Others predicted the time and place of the birth of Jesus Christ, including the fact that He would be born of a virgin of the tribe of Judah. Details of His life, crucifixion, and resurrection were foretold.

It would be impossible to comprehend the mathematical probability of these prophecies coming to pass if they were not inspired by God. Taking just eleven specific prophecies, Peter Stoner found that the probability of their being fulfilled, if not authored by God, was 1 in 5.76×10^{59} (*Evidence That Demands a Verdict*, Josh McDowell).

As convincing as these four testimonies are to the accuracy of the Scripture, the most important testimony is the Bible's internal witness.

What Jesus Thought about the Scriptures

By faith, we accept the fact that the Lord Jesus Christ is the mighty God (Isaiah 9:6). Therefore, we accept His words as the Word of God. What did He say about the authorship, authority, reliability, and nature of the Scriptures?

The Jews, recognizing that Jesus made Himself "equal with God," sought to kill Him. In His answer to them, recorded in John 5:39, 45-47, Jesus established the following facts: (1) There was a real man named Moses; (2) This man Moses wrote a book; (3) Moses wrote of Jesus Christ; (4) All the Scriptures known at the time of Jesus (identical to our Old

Testament today, except for arrangements and divisions of books) testify of Him.

In Luke 20:41-44, Christ attributed some writing from the Psalms to David, indicating, again, that there was a real man by that name, a king of Israel, who wrote some of the psalms.

Jesus extended His endorsement of the Scriptures to another book in Matthew 24:15: there was a man by the name of Daniel, and he wrote the book that is called by his name.

What was Jesus' view of the inspiration of Scripture? He answered that question in Mark 12:36, where He declared that David spoke "by the Holy Ghost." He did not "speak his own mind," nor did he just "write about God." Rather, he spoke by the inspiration and command of the Holy Spirit.

What of the reliability of Scripture? Jesus said, "The scripture cannot be broken" (John 10:35). The Greek word *luo*, translated "broken," carries the literal or figurative meaning of "to loosen." Jesus asserted, then, that the Scriptures are a unit; they stand as one. To divide them at any point in an attempt to identify portions as uninspired or in error would be an attempt to destroy them.

Jesus accredited the entirety of the Scriptures included in the Hebrew manuscripts, of which our Old Testament today is comprised, when He mentioned specifically the three major sections of Old Testament Scripture: (1) the law of Moses; (2) the prophets; (3) the psalms. (See Matthew 7:12; Luke 16:31; 24:44.)

Jesus assigned infallibility to all these Old Testament books when He said, "All things must be fulfilled" (Luke 24:44). These were not the writings of mere men, but of men inspired and moved by the Holy Ghost; they were indeed breathed by God, who knew every detail of the future. (See II Timothy 3:16, II Peter 1:21.)

What the Old Testment Says about Itself

Some 2,500 times, the Old Testament says, "Thus saith the LORD." Other phrases, such as "And God said," and "The word of the Lord came unto me, saying," abound. Without doubt, the Old Testament claims to be the very Word of God. These words are not to be added to or taken away from. (See Deuteronomy 4:2; Proverbs 30:5-6.)

To David, God revealed the permanence of His Word: "For ever, O LORD, thy word is settled in heaven" (Psalm 119:89). This verse seems to speak of the preexistence of the Word as a unit in the mind of God from eternity. There is no changing to the Word of God; once He has spoken, the Word remains the same. While the seasons come and go, His Word stands unmoved throughout the ages (Isaiah 40:8).

What the New Testament Says about Itself

The New Testament accords the highest possible view to the origin of the Scriptures: "All scripture is given by inspiration of God, and is profitable for doctrine, for reproof, for correction, for instruction in righteousness" (II Timothy 3:16). The word translated "inspired" (Greek, *theopneustos*) indicates that Scripture is "God-breathed."

That the will of man had nothing to do with the writing of Scripture is seen in II Peter 1:20-21: "Knowing this first, that no prophecy of the scripture is of any private interpretation. For the prophecy came not in old time by the will of man: but holy men of God spake as they were moved by the Holy Ghost."

The New Testament bears its own internal witness to the inspiration of the books within its scope. Paul claimed to write the commandments of the Lord (I Corinthians 14:37). So did John (Revelation 22:18-19). Peter identified Paul's writings as Scripture

(II Peter 3:15-16). Peter also claimed equal authority for himself and all the apostles with the holy prophets of old (II Peter 3:2). Paul accredited the gospels as Scripture (I Timothy 5:18).

Psalm 119

Psalm 119, a poem to the Word of God, is an acrostic Psalm consisting of twenty-two sections of eight verses each. In each of the sections, every verse begins with the same letter of the Hebrew alphabet. In the first section, every verse begins with the first letter, Aleph. In the second section, each verse begins with the second letter, Beth. Every verse in the third section begins with Gimel, the third letter of the Hebrew alphabet. This pattern continues throughout the psalm, so that each of the twenty-two letters of the Hebrew alphabet is used in order.

The acrostic is a literary device used here and elsewhere in the Hebrew Scriptures (e.g., Proverbs 31:10-31; Lamentations 1-4) as an aid to memory. Psalm 119 is intended to be committed to memory; the ancient Hebrews rightly placed a high value on memorizing Scripture. It is significant that the most elaborate acrostic in the Hebrew Scriptures is itself dedicated to the Word of God.

The individual psalms are categorized into fourteen types, ranging from individual laments to hymns to history. Psalm 119 is one of three psalms identified as Torah, or instruction. (The other two are Psalms 1 and 19.)

The psalms were written over a period of about one thousand years, with the earliest (Psalm 90) written by Moses in about 1410 B.C. The latest were written after Israel's return from exile in Babylon (e.g., Psalm 137). David wrote the greatest number of psalms, about seventy-three, between 1010-971

B.C. Jewish tradition credits Ezra with the final compilation of the psalms; indeed, according to this tradition, Ezra is responsible for Psalm 119.

The central message of Psalm 119 is that a love for and obedience to the Word of God results in blessings. Various terms are used in Psalm 119:97-109 to describe the Word of God. These include "law," "commandments," testimonies," "precepts," "word," and "judgments."

Verse 97. The word "law" is translated from the Hebrew *Torah.* It should not be thought that the psalmist had in mind only the legal code given at Sinai. Although Torah is used today to describe the first five books of the Bible, including the pre-Sinaitic material, this does not mean that the psalmist had in mind only the books of Genesis, Exodus, Leviticus, Numbers, and Deuteronomy when he declared his love for the Torah and his meditation in it. Torah has to do with instruction or teaching, which includes, but is not limited to, the specific laws found in the Pentateuch. In the broadest since, all Hebrew Scripture is Torah and worthy of love and meditation.

Verse 98. The word "commandments" is translated from the Hebrew *Mitzvah.* This word is quite well known, even among Gentiles, because of its use in the Bar-Mitzvah, a Jewish ceremony by means of which a young boy is inducted into manhood. *Bar-Mitzvah* means "a son of the commandment." The use of the term means that the twelve- or thirteen-year old boy is now personally responsible to keep the commandments for himself.

Verse 99. The word "testimonies" is translated from the Hebrew *Eduth,* which refers to the declarations of God Himself in reference to His nature and purpose. The psalmist declared that by meditating on these declarations of God he gains more understanding than that possessed by his human teachers. This should not, of course, be understood to minimize the importance of teachers who are called of God and given to the church in the era of the New Covenant. (See I Corinthians 12:28; Ephesians 4:11.) These teachers are involved in teaching the testimonies of God. The point is simply that God knows more than men and that by meditation upon God's declarations we learn more than could ever be learned by human wisdom.

Verse 100. "Precepts" is translated from the Hebrew *Piqqudim,* a plural word referring to God's charges to man as it relates to man's moral obligations. The psalmist declares that because he adheres to the moral obligations given him by God, he understands more than the ancients. God's precepts far surpass those of the wisest men.

Verse 101. "Word" is translated from the Hebrew *Dabar,* which has to do specifically with speech or utterance and generally with the disclosure of the will of God. The psalmist avoids evil in favor of doing God's will. Evil and the Word of God are mutually incompatible.

Verse 102. "Judgments" is translated from the Hebrew *Mishpat,* a reference to legal pronouncements or rules of divine administration. By means of these pronouncements, the psalmist testifies, God has taught him.

Verse 103. "Words" is translated from the Hebrew *Imrah,* which has to do with a saying or speech. Previously, the psalmist has referred to the value of meditating on the Word of God. (See verses 97, 99.) His claim that the words of God are "sweet" to his taste and "sweeter than honey" to his mouth may refer to vocalizing the words upon which he has meditated. In a figure of speech, he finds these words sweet when spoken.

Verse 104. Again, the psalmist uses *Piqqudim* ("precepts"), a reference to man's God-given moral obligations. In verse 100, he credits the keeping of these precepts as giving him more understanding than that possessed by the wise men of ancient times. Here, he again declares that God's precepts produce understanding. They enable a person to put "every false way" in proper perspective. Without the precepts of God, men would be deceived morally.

Verse 105. Here the psalmist moves from the "Mem" section of his acrostic to the "Nun" section. He declares that the Word (*Dabar*) of God illuminates his steps. (See verse 101.) Since *Dabar* refers, in general, to the disclosure of the divine will, the psalmist means that the will of God serves to give him direction.

Verse 106. The psalmist returns to the use of the word "judgments" (*Mishpat*). (See verse 102.) He has "sworn and confirmed" (NKJV) that he will keep the "righteous judgments" of God. He intends to submit to divine rules.

Verse 107. For the third time in our text, the word *Dabar* is used. The psalmist confesses he is "afflicted very much," and he seeks revival "according unto [God's] word." He has seen in the declarations of God that personal revival is possible in the midst of affliction, and he desires to receive that benefit.

Verse 108. Also for the third time in our text, the psalmist uses *Mishpat* ("judgments") in an appeal to be taught by God. The same word is used in verse 102 to declare that it is by the judgments that the psalmist has been taught. He does not consider himself to have learned all that he needs to know; he yearns for more teaching from the judgments of God.

Verse 109. The psalmist returns to the use of *Torah*. His statement, "My soul is continually in my hand" refers to the uncertainty of life, but even in this precarious state he does not forget the law—the instruction—of God.

Scripture is one aspect of the special revelation given by God. By means of the written Word of God, we learn about God Himself and how to relate to Him. Prior to the giving of the Scriptures, God revealed Himself by means of general revelation. Although general revelation is sufficient to give men a knowledge of God, it does not offer the specific and detailed knowledge of God that comes through His Word.

The Word of God is unique; there is no other book in existence that can compare to it. Wherever it is taught, believed, and lived, it has a positive influence on individual human lives and on society in general.

The trustworthiness of Scripture has been demonstrated by archaeological discoveries and the fulfillment of prophecy. Although the primary purpose of archaeology is not to "prove" Scripture to be reliable, it has nevertheless served that effect. No discovery has ever demonstrated any scriptural claim to be in error. Every prophecy that has been fulfilled has been fulfilled literally, precisely as predicted.

Jesus believed the Scriptures to be the very words of God. The internal testimony of both the Old and New Testaments is that Scripture originates with God; it is inspired of Him and it is not the result of human initiative.

Because Scripture is what it claims to be, it is worthy of the utmost reverence and obedience. Those who hope to live in the Spirit will live according to the Word of God, which resulted from the moving of the Spirit on holy men of old.

Test Your Knowledge

1. What is the difference between general revelation and special revelation?
2. What is meant by the "internal testimony" of Scripture?

3. Discuss Jesus' view of scriptural authority.

4. What does the word "inspired" mean?

5. Define the following words: *Torah*; *Mitzvah*; *Eduth*; *Piqqudim*; *Dabar*; *Mishpat*; *Imrah*.

Apply Your Knowledge

In order to commit yourself to living the Word of God, set a goal of memorizing a portion of Scripture regularly, even if it is only one verse each week. Make yourself accountable to someone; quote the verses to them. In order to maintain your motivation, select passages of Scripture that seem specially meaningful to you at this time.

Expand Your Knowledge

Here is a long-term project that could bear rich rewards. By use of works like *Strong's Exhaustive Concordance* or *Young's Analytical Concordance*, write out all the references in the Hebrew Scriptures where the various words seen in Psalm 119:97-109 are used to describe the Word of God. Does a common theme emerge where the same word is used? When the project is completed, summarize your findings by listing the chief characteristics of Scripture emphasized by each word. Share your findings with your Sunday school class or Bible study group.

Evidence That Demands a Verdict, by Josh McDowell, is a source for further information regarding this subject.

4 Fruit Bearing

But thou, O man of God, flee these things; and follow after righteousness, godliness, faith, love, patience, meekness.

I Timothy 6:11

Start with the Scriptures

John 15
Galatians 5:22-23
II Peter 1:9

Many things set Christianity apart from all the world's religions. One of these is that Christianity teaches an entirely different relationship with God than other religions teach.

All non-Christian religions focus on salvation as a reward for effort; if a person's behavior conforms to specified ethical norms, he may earn salvation. Christianity presents salvation as a gift of God, freely given.

Although the practitioners of both Christianity and non-Christian religions will adopt specific lifestyles, for the non-Christian the lifestyle is part of an attempt to gain favor with God in hopes of meriting salvation. But the Christian lifestyle is a *result* of salvation. The Christian's behavior is not a self-absorbed struggle to measure up to an ethical norm; it is a life of simple yieldedness to the indwelling Holy Spirit.

To the Romans, Paul wrote, "Yield yourselves unto God, as those that are alive from the dead, and your members as instruments of righteousness unto God" (Romans 6:13). He also wrote to the Corinthians, "But by the grace of God I am what I am: and his grace which was bestowed upon me was not in vain; but I laboured more abundantly than they all: yet not I, but the grace of God which was with me" (I Corinthians 15:10).

In short, non-Christian religions teach salvation by works; Christianity teaches salvation by grace through faith and not of works: "For by grace are ye saved through faith; and that not of yourselves: it is the gift of God: not of works, lest any man should boast" (Ephesians 2:8-9).

None of this suggests that the Christian's behavior is unimportant. Indeed, faith without works is dead. (See James 2:14-26.) But the Christian's behavior is not the *cause* of his salvation; it is the *result* of it. Perfectly illustrating this point, Scripture declares that the behavior of a Spirit-filled Christian is the "fruit of the Spirit."

The Fruit of the Spirit

There are natural consequences when the Holy Spirit indwells a believer. These consequences are described in Galatians 5:22-23: "But the fruit of the Spirit is love, joy, peace, longsuffering, gentleness, goodness, faith, meekness, temperance: against such there is no law."

In the immediate context, Paul contrasts the *fruit of the Spirit* with the *works of the flesh*. (See Galatians 5:19-21.) The larger context of the entire letter to the Galatians contrasts the legalistic Old Covenant orientation of the Judaizers (who saw salvation as something earned by good works) to the New Covenant life in the Spirit.

The more perfectly a believer yields to the leading of the Holy Spirit, and the less he depends on his own strength, the more fully the fruit of the Spirit will be demonstrated in his life. (See Galatians 5:25.) Each aspect of the Spirit's fruit reflects the character of God Himself. (See II Peter 1:4-7.) It is important to note that the word "fruit" is singular; where the Spirit rules, all nine characteristics of the Spirit will prevail. Together, they constitute the fruit of the Spirit.

Love

It is appropriate that love heads the list of the various aspects of the Spirit's fruit. Love is the preeminent virtue. (See I Corinthians 13:13.) It is so characteristic of the Holy Spirit Himself that God is identified as love. (See I John 4:8.) The love of God was most strikingly demonstrated by the gift of His Son for the salvation of the world. (See John 3:16.) He gave because He "so loved."

The Greek word *agape*, translated "love," expresses something far more significant than other words used for love in other contexts. The Greek *phileo* refers to brotherly love in the sense of having affection for someone or liking someone, while *eros* has to do with passionate, sensual love. On the other hand, *agape* seems to speak of a more pure, altruistic love that expresses itself in compassionate acts with no thought for personal advantage. Paul describes its characteristics perfectly in I Corinthians 13:4-7. By definition, *agape* is longsuffering, kind, free from envy, self-effacing, humble, polite, others-oriented, not provoked, free from evil thoughts, characterized by rejoicing in truth rather than in iniquity, inclined to bear all things, believing, hopeful, and enduring.

Joy

Where there is genuine love, there will be joy. It is the natural outgrowth of the Holy Spirit. (See I Thessalonians 1:6.) Joy is translated from the Greek *chara*, which is related to *charis* ("graciousness," "favor," "grace") and *charisma* ("a gift freely and graciously given"). Biblical joy does not express the same idea as "happiness" in our present culture. Joy is a deep, inner rejoicing characterizing those who abide in Jesus. (See John 15:11.) The current idea of "happiness" seems to be related to circumstances; joy is not. As with all the fruit of the Spirit, joy is not the result of the believer trying harder to be happy. It is the natural result of trusting in and relying completely and exclusively on Jesus for one's life both in this present world and in the world to come.

Peace

In conjunction with giving His disciples the gift of peace, Jesus offered insight as to the nature of the gift: "Peace I leave with you, my peace I give unto you: not as the world giveth, give I unto you. Let not your heart be troubled, neither let it be afraid" (John 14:27).

Peace is not the absence of conflict; it is an untroubled heart in the midst of the frequent and intense conflicts that occur in a world marred by sin. This untroubled state is reached not by attempting to block out or deny the real world, but by resting in the promise of Jesus to go with us through all our difficulties. (See Matthew 28:20.) Such peace is contrary to human reason. (See Philippians 4:7.)

The kingdom of God is characterized by peace, not by quibbling over such non-essentials as what to eat and what to drink. (See Romans 14:17.) Indeed, believers are to actively pursue a life that results in peaceful relationships with other believers. (See Romans 14:19.)

Longsuffering

Longsuffering has to do with one's response when he is provoked. The indwelling Holy Spirit prompts the believer to accept mistreatment when it is for his Christian testimony. Christ Himself did not revile those who persecuted Him, and those who allow Christ to live through them will do the same. (See Matthew 5:10-12, 38-48; Romans 12:14, 17-21; I Peter 2:21-23.) Paul demonstrated this aspect of the Spirit's fruit himself. (See II Corinthians 6:6.) One who suffers as a Christian is not to be ashamed; he is to glorify God for the privilege of identifying with Christ in this way. (See I Peter 4:16.)

Gentleness

The King James Version translates *chrestotes* as "gentleness." The same word is translated "kindness" by the New King James Version and other more recent English translations. It has to do with the benevolence God has demonstrated to men. The word is translated "goodness" in Romans 2:4 and "kindness" in Ephesians 2:7. In the former reference, it is the "goodness" of God that leads people to repent; in the latter, the "kindness" of God toward us through Christ Jesus is a demonstration of His grace.

Goodness

Goodness has a twofold meaning. First, it speaks of moral excellence or uprightness of soul. Second, it has to do with kindness in action or generosity even toward those who do not deserve it. Paul commended the Roman believers for their goodness. (See Romans 15:14.)

Faith

The "faith" spoken of here is the fruit, or result, of the indwelling Holy Spirit. Since faith is required for a person to come to God (Hebrews 11:6), thus indicating he must have and exercise faith even before receiving the Spirit, we might suppose that Paul's use of *pistis* here has significance beyond the faith required for salvation. In this case, the NKJV translates the word "faithfulness," as do most recent English translations. It seems to have to do with the faithfulness or trustworthiness of a person who is led by the Holy Spirit. The word is used to describe the faithful servant of Luke 16:10-12.

Meekness

The King James Version translates the Greek *prautes* as "meekness." The New King James Version and other recent translations render it "gentleness." It has to do with the ideal attitude one should have when dealing with sinning brethren (Galatians 6:1), when receiving the instruction of God's Word (James 1:21), when correcting the opposition (II Timothy 2:25), or when answering for one's faith in Christ (I Peter 3:15-16). It should characterize the relationship of believers one with another, even when there may be a legitimate complaint. (See Colossians 3:12-13.)

Temperance

Temperance has to do with self-control. The Greek word is found only here and in Acts 24:25 and II Peter 1:6. In the latter reference, Peter lists self-control as something that should be added to knowledge and as something to which should be added perseverance. The idea, especially in the larger context of the letter to the Galatians, seems to be that the life of a Christian is not to be characterized by impulsiveness or self-indulgence. The believer should be self-disciplined, not allowing the impulses of the sin principle to dominate him. This can be done only as one depends on the power of the indwelling Holy Spirit. (See Galatians 5:16.)

No Law Against the Spirit's Fruit

Obviously, the works of the flesh are in opposition to the law of God. (See Galatians 5:19-21.) Those who practice them will not inherit the kingdom of God. Not so with the fruit of the Spirit: "Against such [the fruit of the Spirit] there is no law" (Galatians 5:23). The Old Covenant made many demands upon the people of Israel, but it did nothing to enable them to conform to its requirements. (See Romans 7:5, 8-11, 13; 8:3.) The New Covenant, on the other hand, actually enables the believer to conform to its ethical standards. (See Philippians 2:13.) This is done by the power of the indwelling Holy Ghost.

The Difference Between Gifts and Fruit

The fruit of the Spirit (Galatians 5:22-23) and the gifts of the Spirit (I Corinthians 12:4-11) are two different operations of the Holy Spirit. The carnality of the Corinthians (I Corinthians 3:3-4) did not prevent the gifts from operating. The reason for this is that the gifts of the Spirit are just that: *gifts*. They are not the evidence of spiritual maturity. They do not indicate that the person operating them has achieved advanced spiritual power. This is the difference between *gifts* and *fruit*. The fruit of the Spirit (Galatians 5:22-23) gives evidence of spiritual maturity. The fruit tells us something about the person's character and spirituality. But the gifts tell us nothing about the person's character or spirituality. Instead, they tell us about the nature of the Giver, who is God Himself.

The Vine and the Branches

Jesus described the relationship of the believers to Himself in terms of the relationship between a vine and its branches (John 15). He is the vine; believers are the branches. The branches are totally dependent on the vine for life and productivity. The Father is pictured as the husbandman who dresses the vine for further production. The fruit seems to relate to what Paul later wrote to be the fruit of the Spirit (Galatians 5:22-23).

As the vine, Jesus is the source of life for the branches. The branches represent the disciples of Jesus. Just as a branch is fully dependent on the vine for life and productivity, so the followers of Jesus are fully dependent on Him for their life and their ability to bear fruit.

The vine and branches figure is not original in John 15. Several Old Testament references compare the relationship between Israel and Jehovah similarly. (See Psalm 80:8-16; Isaiah 5:1-7; Jeremiah 2:21; 6:9; 12:10; Ezekiel 15; 17; and Hosea 10:1.) These references are essentially negative, however, referring to the spiritual fruitlessness and decay of the nation of Israel.

Even in this New Testament metaphor, the possibility of fruitlessness is recognized. However, the emphasis is on the potential for fruit-bearing as the branches stay securely in the vine, allowing its life-giving energy to flow through them.

While Jesus is the vine, He said, "My Father is the husbandman" (John 15:1). The husbandman is the vine dresser, or farmer, who is responsible for the care of the vineyard.

A trinitarian interpretation of John 15:1 would perhaps see it as an indication of two persons in the Godhead. The Oneness perspective, however, sees this as another indication of both the humanity and deity of the Messiah, Jesus Christ.

Just as Jesus could be both a Shepherd and a Door in the same parable (John 10:9, 11), He could be both the vine and the vine dresser in this.

This should not be taken as a reference to two co-equal persons in the Godhead, both sharing in the same deity but with different functions. As seen in the metaphor, the vine and the husbandman are not of the same nature.

Doctrines are not based on metaphors or parables. They are based on theological passages specifically addressing the doctrine under consideration. Doctrine concerning the identity of Christ is clearly declared in passages like I Timothy 3:16, where He is seen as "God . . . manifest in the flesh."

Jesus' references to His Father should be understood in the larger context of His life on earth as an authentic man (the Word [God] made flesh, John 1:1,14). Although Jesus was in the form (Greek, *morphe*, emphasizing attributes of deity but recognizing a visible appearance) of God and was thus equal with God (e.g., He *was* God), He humbled Himself by giving up His reputation, taking on a servant's form, a human body, and surrendering to death by crucifixion. (See Philippians 2:5-8).

As the Messiah, Jesus is the true vine. He is not involved, as the Messiah, in the pruning process. His anointed messianic ministry was one of healing, delivering, and preaching good news, not pruning. Pruning is a function of deity.

Increasing Fruit

In Jesus' parable of the vine and branches, He indicates the possiblity of four levels of fruitfulness: (1) Some branches bear no fruit at all. (2) Some bear fruit. (3) There is the possibility of bearing more fruit. (4) Some bear much fruit (John 15:2, 5, 8).

The essential requirement for bearing fruit is to abide in Jesus (John 15:4, 6), just as a branch abides in the vine. In this case, the relationship of the branch to the vine seems to be a metaphor for believing, or for trusting exclusively and completely, in Jesus Christ for one's salvation and fruitfulness. Those who abide in His love will demonstrate that by keeping His commandments. (See John 15:10.) Contextually, this means loving others. (See John 15:12.) In other words, those who abide in Jesus will allow His life to flow through them, just as the life of the vine flows through the branches. Since He loves, they will love. Since He is full of joy, so will they be. (See John 15:11.)

It would be a mistake to think that the key to increased fruitfulness is for the believer to try harder to be loving, or joyous, or peaceful, or longsuffering, or kind, or good, or faithful, or gentle, or temperate. This is to focus on precisely the wrong thing. It is to put the proverbial cart before the horse. Sanctification, or practical holiness, is not worked out in the believer's life by mere self-discipline. It is, rather, the result of yieldedness to the impulses of the Holy Ghost.

The advice given by Paul to those who would produce spiritual fruit and avoid the works of the flesh puts this in perspective: "This I say then, Walk in the

Spirit, and ye shall not fulfil the lust of the flesh. . . . If we live in the Spirit, let us also walk in the Spirit" (Galatians 5:16, 25).

To the Romans, Paul gave similar counsel: "For if ye live after the flesh, ye shall die: but if ye through the Spirit do mortify the deeds of the body, ye shall live. For as many as are led by the Spirit of God, they are the sons of God" (Romans 8:13-14).

But life in the Spirit does not follow the pattern of life in the flesh. The spiritual life is the natural result of dependence on Jesus Christ. To be led by the Spirit is to respond to the promptings of the Holy Spirit. To give evidence of spiritual fruit, we must abide in Jesus—keep trusting in and relying upon Him exclusively—and allow Him to live His life through us.

Though the gifts of the Spirit and the fruit of the Spirit are both manifestations of the same Holy Spirit, they are two distinct works. The gifts of the Spirit are freely given, without regard for spiritual maturity. The fruit of the Spirit, however, demonstrates the degree of one's yieldedness to the Holy Spirit.

Test Your Knowledge

1. As discussed in this lesson, what is one of the things that sets Christianity apart from other religions of the world?

2. Can you list all nine aspects of the fruit of the Spirit, in order?

3. Why does Paul refer to these nine characteristics as fruit, rather than fruits, of the Spirit?

4. Define as many of the nine aspects of the fruit of the Spirit as you can.

5. What does it mean to abide in the vine?

6. Explain the relationship between Jesus as the vine and the Father as the husbandman in Oneness terms.

7. What can a person do to bear more fruit?

Apply Your Knowledge

As clearly as you can, write on one sheet of paper the teaching of a non-Christian religion as to how a person can be saved. Contrast this with the teaching of Scripture that we are saved by grace through faith.

Examine your own life to see if you are struggling in one or more of the areas of the fruit of the Spirit. What can you do, other than trying harder, to see improvement in this area of your Christian life?

It is possible that some aspects of the fruit of the Spirit may be latent or potential, rather than active, in your life. Look for opportunities to put these aspects of the fruit to work. Specifically, is there someone to whom you can show kindness, goodness, or gentleness? You should not have to look far for these opportunities.

Expand Your Knowledge

No one demonstrated the fruit of the Spirit more perfectly than Jesus. Choose one of the Gospels to read completely through. But this time, look specifically at Jesus' life and ministry for evidence of the fruit of the Spirit, and mark each verse where He exhibits love, joy, peace, longsuffering, kindness, goodness, faithfulness, gentleness, and self-control. Devise a code as to which characteristic He exhibits, and make a chain of texts so that you can locate each demonstration of love, of joy, and so on. A study Bible may make this assignment easier.

Your public library should have a book on vine dressing. See what insights it would offer on the parable of the vine and branches of John 15.

5 Spiritual Reproduction

The fruit of the righteous is a tree of life; and he that winneth souls is wise.

Proverbs 11:30

It is a simple picture. Two boats are standing idle and empty by the Sea of Galilee. A crowd of people are pressing closer to the edge of the lake to hear an itinerant preacher. The preacher moves, stepping purposefully into one of the boats. Peter is there and pushes the boat out a little distance from the shore.

Over the calm waters a strong voice speaks of hope and heaven. The voice carries well. It reaches the hearts of the hundreds who stand listening at the lakeside.

When the preacher finishes speaking He turns to Peter. He does not request; He commands, "Launch out into the deep, and let down your nets for a draught" (Luke 5:4). The fisherman obeys, though he and his partners have worked all night and have taken nothing. He obeys, though fishing in the shallows is the usual way. Peter obeys, entranced by the words of the One who has sat next to him in the fishing boat.

The nets have been washed and mended. They are ready to be hung up and dried. Just one more effort, just one more throw, Peter thinks to himself. He leans hard over the edge of the ship as he throws out his net. There is a sudden swirling in the water, a sudden drag on the line. Peter braces himself and barely holds on. The nets are full of fish. There is a frantic call for the partners in the other boat. Strong hands pull in the catch. Water is splashing. Fins are flashing. Both boats are at the point of sinking.

God was in that fishing boat. The Almighty was in a little ship. He was among men as the Son of man, as God manifested in flesh "reconciling the world unto himself" (II Corinthians 5:19).

Peter was humbled and astonished, amazed at the draught of fishes. He caught something of the marvel of the moment and heard the gracious words of Christ: "Fear not; from henceforth thou shalt catch men" (Luke 5:10).

Peter and his partners, James and John, ran their ships on shore. They left the nets, the catch, and the fishing boats. They left behind everything to follow Jesus.

Forsaking All

What caused these men to suddenly forsake all? Albert Barnes commented, "It was not much that they left—a couple of small boats and their nets: but it was all they had, even all their living." Obviously "forsaking all" was a condition of discipleship. Jesus always expected supreme loyalty from those who followed Him. Family relationships and personal interests had to take second place to His cause. A tremendous cost was involved, and as He fore-warned the multitude, a cross had to be borne. "So likewise," Jesus admonished, "whosoever he be of you that forsaketh not all that he hath, he cannot be my disciple" (Luke 14:33).

The summons to become "fishers of men" was no ordinary calling. Christ's "henceforth" (which means "from now on") showed that He expected an imme-diate change in these men's interests. Delay on the part of the disciples was unacceptable. The net-breaking miracle on the sea had illustrated the fact that God could bless their efforts beyond their wildest imaginations. The only question was whether they would fervently follow Jesus.

It certainly must have seemed to the disciples that they had "launched out into the deep." As they walked daily with the Master, there must have been a good deal of uncertainty in their minds. The crowds were encouraging, the miracles exhilarating, but Jesus did have the habit of stirring up contro-versy wherever He went. He just did not fit in with the traditions of the day. He spoke boldly against the excesses of the Pharisees and openly showed that He loved the social outcasts. He welcomed the beg-gars, the publicans, and the prostitutes. He came to all people, whoever they were and however sinful.

The disciples must have continually wondered at the Lord Jesus. If He was who He claimed to be—the Son of God—then why would He be concerned with lepers? Why would He permit His enemies to brazenly attack and defame Him? How could He allow a woman with an issue of blood to touch His garments and a Roman centurion to take His time?

Jesus wanted His disciples to know that He would

identify with anyone who looked to Him for deliverance. There were no sins too great for His forgiveness. The Lord went out of His way to minister to the most hopeless cases—the people whom all others had rejected. His whole ministry was an expression of love to the hurting and the helpless. He wanted us all to know how deeply He cared.

The Difference

There was a vast difference between Christ and His disciples. He was the shepherd; they were the sheep. He was driven by a mission; they followed along, not quite understanding His purpose. One day, while the disciples were gone to buy food, Jesus talked to a Samaritan woman about her need of salvation. On their return, the disciples encouraged the Lord to eat, but He seemed strangely preoccupied. "I have meat to eat," He told them, "that ye know not of" (John 4:32).

The salvation of souls was the Lord's consuming passion. In His parables He talked to men about the kingdom of God and its growth; in His discourses He told them of a new relationship they could have with God and with one another. His prayer request was that the Lord of the harvest would send forth laborers into the fields. His intercession for others, however, was so powerful that the disciples asked of Him, "Teach us to pray" (Luke 11:1).

Other men had espoused noble causes. They also had been sincere in wanting to improve the lives of others. Some had even given their lives as a sacrifice for the ideals that they upheld. The difference was that Jesus was God manifest in the flesh. (See I Timothy 3:16; John 1:1, 14.)

Love and compassion flowed from Jesus as naturally as rivers into an ocean. Luke wrote in Acts 10:38 that the Lord "went about doing good, and healing all that were oppressed of the devil." The disciples saw His concern for a whole city as He wept over Jerusalem, and they saw His compassion for one friend as He wept at the tomb of Lazarus. There was something wonderfully transparent about Christ's love. It was rich; it was full; it was free.

With a touch of the Spirit upon their lives, the seventy whom Jesus sent out were able to take charge of demons. How much more effectively would His followers be able to minister after they had received the Holy Ghost! (See Mark 16:16-18.) Jesus told His disciples, "It is expedient for you that I go away: for if I go not away, the Comforter will not come unto you" (John 16:7). He knew better than any other just how much they needed His love and His power.

Calvary appeared as a colossal defeat to the disciples; it took forty days for the resurrected Christ to convince them that it was a colossal victory. The price for sin had now been paid. What seemed to be an ending was just a beginning. Had Jesus not said, "Except a corn of wheat fall into the ground and die, it abideth alone: but if it die, it bringeth forth much fruit" (John 12:24)? And there would be much fruit.

There would be tremendous growth and reproduction after Christ's departure, but it would not occur until the disciples were filled with the Spirit. They were not to go out and preach until the Day of Pentecost was fully come. Then, as a great stone strikes the surface of a lake, the waves would flow outward from Jerusalem. The Spirit would flow into Judea, Samaria, and into the uttermost corners of the world.

Love Will Find a Way

These are stressful days. It seems that more and more people are frazzled and frustrated, disillusioned and disappointed. Thousands are desperately sick of their loveless marriages or their sinful relationships. Some are no longer pretending they can cope with their situations. Many turn to drugs or alcohol. Some try to find satisfaction in the occult. In a mad dash for some kind of freedom, others rebel against every moral standard they can think of.

These people are reaching for reality. If their lifestyles shock us, we must realize that hidden below their rough surfaces are souls for whom Christ died. He came to save the lonely, the least, and the lost.

Love will find a way. Love will manifest itself when all else has failed. It will reach out with a kind word here or a sincere action there. "Its hopes," Paul the apostle stated, "are fadeless under all circumstances and it endures everything [without weakening]" (I Corinthians 13:7, *The Amplified Bible*). Love for souls must express itself or it will die.

There are no pat answers when seeking souls. There are no foolproof methods or flawless routines. But sinners will sense it when we genuinely love them. They may not understand all of our doctrine, but they can feel much of our concern. They will know the difference between those who are trying to win them to "a religion" and those who have a Christ-like burden for them as individuals.

If we follow Christ's example, we will inconvenience ourselves for the lost. We will show an interest in their problems and make ourselves available to their needs. New converts, we must realize, are especially challenged. They must turn their backs on much of their old lifestyle. Indeed, they face a strong possibility of losing their friends or their jobs. Effective soulwinning demands a great deal of perseverance and wisdom. "He that winneth souls is wise" (Proverbs 11:30).

Soulwinning should come naturally to us as Christians. We now have the Spirit of Christ. We have a new nature, unlike the old nature that is self-ish and hateful. The Holy Ghost within our hearts strongly urges us to share our joy and to reproduce ourselves in those around us.

And what do we really mean by soulwinning?

Soulwinning is Paul, a former Pharisee, warning everyone "night and day with tears" (Acts 20:31). It is Lydia, a dealer in fabrics, first opening her heart to the gospel and then opening her home to those who preached the gospel. It is Priscilla and Aquila, tentmakers, befriending Paul and leading Apollos to a greater understanding of the Scriptures. It is the Samaritan woman, leaving her waterpot—as well as her sinful past—to publicize, "Come, see a man, which told me all things that ever I did: is not this the Christ?" (John 4:29).

Although gospel literature is informative for those who are searching, it will never take the place of a personal testimony. Your one-to-one contact is all-important. People need a friend, someone who will meet them where they are living. They need a listening ear and a responsive heart. A newcomer, like a newborn child, must have the support of one or more individuals. Even Paul the apostle needed the friendship and the backing of Barnabas.

Are home Bible studies important? Yes, they most certainly are, but even this tool will fail if there is no burden for the lost. If the kingdom of God is to be extended, somehow we must realize the urgency of the hour. There may be times when all our preconceived plans will have to be set aside. Our charts and our notes may not fit the current need. The Spirit may lead differently. We may hear an unusual but pressing cry from a soul.

The Handicapped

"And there were four leprous men at the entering

in of the gate: and they said one to another, Why sit we here until we die?" (II Kings 7:3).

Who could have imagined that the Lord would use four lepers to bring about an outstanding deliverance? All, of course, was uniquely in the hands of God, but the situation looked hopeless. The lepers were at the point of death as they sat by the gate of the famine-stricken city. They were not only physically handicapped, they were also social outcasts.

But the need of the lepers was so great that it caused these spectres of humanity to do something. They discussed the situation and came up with a common question, "Why sit we here until we die?" (II Kings 7:3).

While some might insist upon the term "physically challenged," most of us know what is meant by the word "handicapped." We have seen those blue parking signs with a white wheelchair painted on them. Those signs indicate that a special effort is being made to provide for the physically disabled. Someone who cared felt that the disadvantaged needed to have some advantage.

In a very real sense we have all been handicapped. We have all been spiritually handicapped by sin. If we have been wise, like the four lepers, we have left the place of death and found a place of banqueting and abundance. Our enemies have been despoiled by Christ. "Having spoiled principalities and powers, he made a shew of them openly, triumphing over them in it" (Colossians 2:15).

For a time the lepers reveled in their unexpected riches. They "did eat and drink, and carried thence silver, and gold, and raiment, and went and hid it" (II Kings 7:8). But gradually the four realized that hiding their blessings was mean and selfish. "Then they said one to another, We do not well: this day is a day of good tidings, and we hold our peace" (II Kings 7:9).

Think for a moment of the four lepers hurrying

back to the city of Samaria. In their physical weakness they may have stumbled as they traveled the road back home. They may have felt exhausted. But all that hardly seemed to matter now. They carried some wonderful news. If they bore any booty at all, there would be nothing more welcome to the starving Israelites than a few samples of food. And what a lesson for us today! Believers have nothing better to offer dying sinners than a message of hope and the fruit of the Spirit.

A famine is in the land. Emotionally-wounded people are all around us. It may be hard for the elite of this world to believe, but we have some incredibly good news. It is not right to be silent. "If we tarry till the morning light, some mischief will come upon us" (II Kings 7:9).

How powerfully this should speak to the complacent Christian! The typical activity of the day is to be eating and drinking. (See Matthew 24:38.) The impelling need of the hour is to be going and telling. Legion, the man delivered from demons, was instructed by Christ, "Go home to thy friends, and tell them how great things the Lord hath done for thee, and hath had compassion on thee" (Mark 5:19). Similarly, the disciples were instructed in the great commission, "Go ye into all the world, and preach the gospel to every creature" (Mark 16:15).

Can God use the handicapped? Can He use those of us who grapple with fears and inhibitions? Will He manifest Himself to us, though we struggle to lean upon His promises?

The answer can be found in the Scriptures. There we find an impressive array of handicapped individuals whom God used in mighty ways.

- There was Jacob, who met an angel on his return from Haran and wrestled all night. He gained a great spiritual victory but only after his thigh was put out of joint.

- Another with a disadvantage was Moses. He became God's great spokesman to Israel. Before this, however, he was thoroughly convinced that he was unable to express himself properly. "I am slow of speech," he had admitted, "and of a slow tongue" (Exodus 4:10).
- Ruth would become a forebearer of David, and through him the Messiah. She had what seemed an insurmountable handicap. She was a Moabitess, born on the wrong side of the Dead Sea.
- Jephthah slew the oppressive Ammonites "with a very great slaughter" (Judges 11:33). His disadvantage had been social. He had been thrown out of his home by his half brothers because his mother was a harlot.
- Paul the apostle wrote the majority of the New Testament epistles and left an outstanding testimony. God, however, allowed him to suffer a thorn in the flesh.

Joy Comes in the Morning

Did you hear that sound? It came from Abram's tent, and it was unmistakably the voice of Sarah. She was laughing for joy. Her happiness seemed boundless. She was laughing and worshiping God at the same time. Her joy was infectious. Others joined in the celebration. The most somber of her friends had to smile. Well past the age of normal childbearing, Sarah had given birth to Isaac, the son of promise. "God hath made me to laugh," Sarah rejoiced, "so that all that hear will laugh with me" (Genesis 21:6).

Sarah's experience demonstrates what the Lord does for those who win a soul. God shares a little of His own joy with us. We join in with heaven's celebration. (See Luke 15:7, 10.) It is "fitting to make merry, to revel and feast and rejoice" (Luke 15:32,

The Amplified Bible). Someone who was dead is alive; someone who was lost is found!

Is it strange, then, that God's servants often weep as they sow the seed of the gospel? No, and there are several good reasons why workers should weep.

First, we know that salvation was purchased at an awful cost, with the precious blood of Jesus Christ. How can we be unmoved by the events of Calvary? Such superlative love touches the heartstrings. Our tears are a fitting expression of the gratitude we feel for Christ's redeeming sacrifice.

Then, too, the believer realizes that he must also be willing to sacrifice if souls are to be won. The work of the gospel demands our very best. The personal cost can be tremendous, and pain is always involved. Disappointments come all too often. Jesus Himself was "a man of sorrows, and acquainted with grief" (Isaiah 53:3).

Often the sower weeps because he feels the burden of Christ for the unsaved. His heart is broken for their lost condition, and he becomes a man driven by a passion for souls. Tears flow when words become inadequate by themselves.

Yet sowing the good seed ultimately brings a great reward. "Weeping may endure for a night, but joy cometh in the morning" (Psalm 30:5). The hour is late, the harvest field is white, and God has given us some inestimable promises. "He that goeth forth and weepeth, bearing precious seed, shall doubtless come again with rejoicing, bringing his sheaves with him" (Psalm 126:6).

To lead people out of sin into a glorious relationship with Jesus Christ is the foremost calling of the church. It is our most important duty and our highest privilege. There is no greater harvest than the harvest of souls. The faithful will one day hear those gracious words, "Well done, thou good and faithful servant" (Matthew 25:21).

Test Your Knowledge

1. What lessons was Jesus teaching His disciples through the miraculous draught of fishes?
2. How do we know that Christ wants our very best?
3. How was Jesus different in His attitude towards the needy?
4. Why was the Lord concerned with lepers and others who seemingly had nothing to offer His cause?
5. Comment on the Scripture, "If we tarry till the morning light, some mischief will come upon us" (II Kings 7:9).
6. Can God use the disadvantaged in His kingdom?
7. What is heaven's reaction to the winning of one soul? What is your reaction?
8. Give reasons why we should weep over souls.

Apply Your Knowledge

Usually the best place to start to witness is at home, among those who love us. Our family members are the ones who know us best, and what a dramatic change they should sense in our lives! There should be many opportunities to share our faith in Christ without being offensive. Even here, however, "he that winneth souls is wise" (Proverbs 11:30). Our relatives and our close friends need to see that a genuine love for Christ brings joy and satisfaction.

Expand Your Knowledge

Read Oswald J. Smith's *The Passion for Souls* (Marshall, Morgan & Scott, Ltd., London, Edinburgh). The late Dr. Smith carried a burden for missions that affected thousands both in North America and abroad.

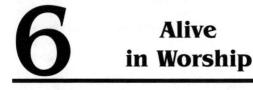

6

Alive in Worship

God is a Spirit: and they that worship him must worship him in spirit and in truth.

John 4:24

Certain characteristics are found in people of all cultures and in every period of civilization. Among these are a recognition of a supreme being and a desire to worship this entity. Even the most pagan of societies, which have never read the Scriptures, have an inborn acknowledgment of God and realize that He deserves worship. How much more should we who have come to know God through His grace and the infilling of His Spirit dedicate ourselves to sincere worship!

Worship is defined in the *Random House College Dictionary* as "reverent honor and homage paid to God or a sacred patronage." From a scriptural viewpoint, worship is not specifically defined, but rather illustrated. According to *Vine's Expository Dictionary of New Testament Words*, worship "includes but is not confined to praise. It is broadly regarded as direct acknowledgment to God of His nature, attributes, ways, and claims; whether by the outgoing of the heart in praise and thanksgiving or by deed done in such acknowledgment."

The trend in our current North American culture seems to be away from genuine gratitude. A business owner recently remarked that he had given 175 turkeys to his employees at Christmas. Only four of those employees even told him "thank you." As Christians we must carefully avoid letting this attitude of our age affect us and steal our worship. Wholehearted worship is essential to a close relationship with the Lord and a key to living a victorious life in Christ.

In this chapter we want to examine the Word of God and see what it has to say about the necessity of worship, how it should be done, who is involved, and the rewards that accompany worship. But beyond intellectual knowledge, our hearts must become involved as we fall in love with Jesus all over again, for we must worship him "in spirit and in truth" (John 4:23).

Why Should We Worship?

Without question God deserves our worship. Isaiah had a revelation of the Lord upon His throne and the angels were crying, "Holy, holy, holy, is the LORD of hosts: the whole earth is full of his glory" (Isaiah 6:3). The angelic beings with their higher status and elevated understanding feel the need to magnify the Lord. Man also possesses this same innate awareness. Part of our creative purpose is to glorify our Creator.

The attributes of the majesty of God are sufficient reason for us to worship Him. Basically we should worship Him because He is God. The ways of the Lord are far above our ways. We operate within the limited confines of time and human ability and sometimes tend to forget the limitless glory of the One Isaiah called "Wonderful." His greatness, splendor, and magnificence all call for our adoration.

In the beginning there was already God. He is the Alpha and Omega, the First and Last. There was none before Him, nor will there be any after Him. Customarily we honor our elders, and rightfully so, recognizing their labors before us and the heritage they have given us. How much more should we honor the Eternal One who dwells in infinity and His days are from everlasting to everlasting?

We should magnify the Lord because He is all-powerful, all-wise, and ever-present. There is nothing so great that He cannot do it, nothing so hard that He does not know the answer, and there is no place that God in His power and wisdom is unable to reach us. Paul stated it beautifully in Romans 11:33: "O the depth of the riches both of the wisdom and knowledge of God! how unsearchable are his judgments, and his ways past finding out!"

It is not only the majesty of God but His revealed power that demands our praise. The creation story is related to us in a few short verses, but the power that is displayed is overwhelming. By just speaking the word, God created the awesome phenomenon called light. Racing into existence at 186,000 miles per second, providing illumination and life, and confounding scientists, this powerful force of light was subdued again by the word of God as He divided light from darkness.

Throughout the creation account we marvel at the power of our God. We see His power demonstrated through many miracles in which He altered the course of the very universe He had set in motion. It was the power of the Creator that caused the Red Sea to part, made the sun stand still, and at the command of the prophet even made the iron head of an axe to float. Such power deserves our worship.

But on a far more personal level, God deserves our worship because of love divine. The pagans feel the necessity to appease their gods because they believe their false gods have power, and they fear that evil will befall them if they do not worship. But we worship our God because we have discovered His love for us.

The greatest story of all time is how the majestic, all-powerful God of eternity chose to become the sacrifice for sin and our Savior. "For ye know the grace of our Lord Jesus Christ, that, though he was rich, yet for your sakes he became poor, that ye through his poverty might be rich" (II Corinthians 8:9).

The ultimate love of our Savior for us is found in that He laid down His life for us—the greatest possible demonstation of love. We have been forgiven, delivered, brought into the body of Christ, loaded with daily blessings, and promised eternal life. In view of such unselfish love, constant worship should flow from our lives.

When Should We Worship?

Worship must become a constant, vital part of the life of every child of God. It is not an activity reserved for a formal church service, but is an attitude affecting all aspects of our lives. Reverence should fill our thoughts, gratitude should flow from our hearts, and praise should be on our lips. A short but powerful verse of Scripture would serve well as our motto: "Rejoice evermore" (I Thessalonians 5:16).

King David attained a place of affection in the heart of God, and much of the credit can go to David's dedication to worship. From his beginning as a shepherd boy, throughout the peaks and valleys of his life as he rose to prominence, David preached and practiced a life of praise to the Lord. Hiding in the cave from Saul, raided by the Amalekites at Ziklag, and dancing in the street as king before the ark of God, this man lived a life of worship unto the Lord. After God had delivered him from Abimelech David sang, "I will bless the LORD at all times: his praise shall continually be in my mouth" (Psalm 34:1).

Worship is not something that is predicated on circumstances. We do not worship God because we feel like it. Nor do we refrain from worship just because we do not feel like it. We worship our Lord because of who He is and what He has done. God is still God, and He is still our Savior, regardless of how we may or may not feel. The psalmist illustrated the need to give praise regardless of the situation when he wrote in Psalm 119:62, "At midnight I will rise to give thanks unto thee."

The beloved apostle John was taken prisoner and cast into exile on the island of Patmos. The natural human reaction would have been to moan and groan and feel sorry for himself. He was being unjustly persecuted while endeavoring to do the work of God. But in Revelation 1:10 John "was in the Spirit on the Lord's day." The pressure of outside forces could not take away the burning inner desire to enter into the presence of the Spirit through worship. This led him to a glorious revelation of Jesus Christ as no other person had ever seen Him.

When should we worship God? Always. For He is always worthy to receive glory, and we will always be blessed when we give Him the glory that is due Him.

How Should We Worship?

True worship must begin with an attitude of reverence. The angels of Isaiah's vision covered their faces in the presence of the Lord. It was an act of reverent respect, just as when Moses removed his shoes before the burning bush. Awe will fill our hearts when we come to see God in His majesty and marvel at His love and kindness to us.

While worship begins with reverence, it is far more than just an attitude. Psalm 149:1-4 describes worship as joyful, exuberant, vocal, demonstrative, and beautiful. Seven times in the Book of Psalms we are exhorted to "shout unto God for joy." Twice in these passages we are instructed to "praise him in the dance." The concept that worship is relegated to some formal, mournful silence is contradictory to the Word of God. Psalm 66:1 and Psalm 100:1 both begin with the exhortation to "make a joyful noise" unto the Lord.

Throughout history mankind has attempted to refine and institutionalize religion. Often he has substituted cold rituals for the unrestrained, joyful response of the soul toward God. But the psalmist and other writers of the Bible would have felt right at home in the atmosphere of Pentecostal praise. Psalm 47 speaks of clapping, shouting, and singing in worship to the Lord most high. Jesus and His disciples sang together only hours before His crucifixion, and Paul wrote to the New Testament churches that they should encourage themselves with psalms, hymns, and spiritual songs. Psalm 150 refers to the use of many musical instruments in offering praise to God and ends with the glorious charge, "Let everything that hath breath praise the LORD. Praise ye the LORD."

Worship extends beyond an attitude of the heart and involves vocal praise to God. This is illustrated in David's prayer in Psalm 51:15, "O LORD, open thou my lips; and my mouth shall shew forth thy praise." His heart was yearning for restoration of fellowship with God, and David's response was to offer praise aloud unto the Lord.

Worship involves demonstrative praise, but it touches many other activities and areas of our lives as well. Service in the kingdom of God can be an act of worship. If our labors are motivated by love and the glory and honor is given to the Lord, then we have worshiped. God can receive glory from even the most menial task if it is done with the proper attitude. Jesus said there would be a reward for those who so much as gave a glass of water to a child of God.

We can also worship the Lord through the proper use of our finances. We should give tithes and offerings with a heart of thankfulness. The apostle Paul wrote in II Corinthians 9:7, "God loveth a cheerful giver."

When we pray with faith in the name of Jesus Christ, we know He hears us and will answer us, and God is glorified. (See John 14:13-14.) The exercise of obedient faith is, in reality, an act of worship. The entire life that we live as disciples of Christ, from spontaneous praise to daily faithfulness, should be a demonstration of unreserved worship.

Who Should Worship?

Perhaps we might be tempted at times to say that we are not the type to engage in worshipful activities. We might feel that it applies to other folks but not to us. But Moses charged all of Israel concerning worship: "And thou shalt rejoice before the LORD thy God, thou, and thy son, and thy daughter, and thy manservant, and thy maidservant, and the Levite that is within thy gates, and the stranger, and the fatherless, and the widow, that among you, in the place which the LORD thy God hath chosen to place his name there" (Deuteronomy 16:11). He was saying that worship is for everyone regardless of age, social status, or personal situation.

Psalm 150:6 declares that everything that has breath should praise the Lord. It is the duty, the purpose, and the privilege of every person to offer sincere, heartfelt praise to God. No exceptions or exemptions are mentioned. If we have breath in our bodies, we are to praise Him.

When we begin to acknowledge the multitude of God's blessings in our lives, thankfulness fills our hearts. The natural expression of the thankful heart is to offer thanksgiving to the Giver of all good things. A legend tells of two angels who were sent to earth. Each angel had a basket. One was to gather all the petitions of men; the other was to gather all the thanks. The legend says that the angel gathering petitions soon returned with a full basket, but the angel collecting prayers of thanksgiving had a basket that was only half full. The sobering truth is that this legend is too often a true description of our prayers.

True gratitude brings joy and liberty to a Christian, but an unthankful heart steals a person's victory. This is clearly illustrated in Deuteronomy 28:47-48. The children of Israel were told that if they failed to serve God with joyfulness and gladness of heart in return for His blessings, then captivity would befall them. Obviously the secret to continued liberty was to give thanks from a joyful heart.

Lest anyone should think that advanced age or spiritual seniority excludes one from the need to worship, we are given the example of Jacob in Scripture. Hebrews 11:21 records that when he was dying, Jacob worshiped God, leaning on the top of his staff. The Book of Genesis concludes that Jacob was 147 years old when he died. After almost a century and a half of living, this man still had a desire to worship God!

When a person is born again of water and the Spirit, he enters into a special relationship with the Lord. While everything with breath should praise Him, those who have been filled with His Spirit enjoy a unique position of praise. We honor Him as Redeemer, Savior, and Life-giver. We are called out to give praise and honor to Him! "But ye are a chosen generation, a royal priesthood, an holy nation, a peculiar people; that ye should shew forth the praises of him who hath called you out of darkness into his marvellous light" (I Peter 2:9).

What Is the Reward of Worship?

The wonderful thing about worship is that even as it glorifies God to whom it is directed, it also blesses the one who is giving the worship. The Scriptures list many benefits that come to the person who worships.

Praise and worship creates a dwelling place for God. Psalm 22:3 says that the Lord inhabits the praises of Israel. When God's people begin to lift up true worship to Him, He dwells in their midst. What greater reward could we possibly receive than to have created a place for God to dwell among us?

Solomon built a marvelous Temple as a place of worship. The Temple was filled with gold and impressive artisanship. But in spite of all of its ornamentation, it was just another building until praise and worship transformed it into the habitation of the Almighty. II Chronicles 5:13-14 lets us know that when unified praise was lifted to heaven, the glory of God came in like a cloud and filled the Temple.

Another benefit of worship is that it gets the attention of heaven. Mark 14 tells of a meal at which Jesus was a guest. In the middle of the formalities a lady came with an expensive box of precious ointment. She broke the box and poured the contents on the head of Jesus. Those present who did not understand worship harshly criticized the woman. But Jesus rebuked them and gave a startling utterance: "Wheresoever this gospel shall be preached throughout the whole world, this also that she hath done shall be spoken of for a memorial of her" (Mark 14:9). A sincere act of sacrificial worship had become the focus of heaven.

Psalm 37:4 promises, "Delight thyself also in the LORD; and he shall give thee the desires of thine heart." We are quick to rush to the second part of the verse and ask for the desires of our heart. But the promise is to those who have caught the attention of heaven by delighting themselves in the Lord.

Worship can sustain the soul during the inevitable storms of life. The Bible makes several references to the song in the night that God can give. Times of darkness and uncertainty try all men. In these difficult times, when answers are scarce and the way is unclear, the song of praise in our souls will carry us through.

Roger Welsch, a folklorist, wrote of research he had done concerning the early settlers on the Great Plains. Numerous photographs and other references revealed that the canary was a frequent part of these pioneers lives. Plunged into a harsh, hostile environment, struggling to establish a homestead, the women of these households suffered the most. But to be able to hear the joyful song of the canary was a source of strength that enabled these brave souls to endure. In the same sense, a song of joy and hope can empower embattled Christians to endure the night and rejoice in the glory of the morning.

Worship leads to victory. Psalm 149:6-9 declares that the high praises of God in the mouth of His children would cause them to triumph over their enemies. At Jericho Joshua led the Israelites to their first victory in Canaan based on worship to the Lord. They sang, they marched, they shouted, and God fought the battle.

Jehoshaphat also led Judah in a battle against seemingly insurmountable odds. The battle plan was certainly unconventional. But with the singers and musicians leading the way in worship, God's people marched to glorious conquest.

One other benefit of worship is that it becomes a witness to the world about us. When we praise God in spite of our circumstances, a powerful message is sent to the lost. The world can understand singing when a person is happy, but a Christian can sing in the storm. This demonstation of faith and confidence in God becomes a vital part of our testimony. According to Nehemiah 12:43, when God's children began to worship and rejoice, the joy of Jerusalem was heard "even afar off." There is a world that is watching, and when we lift up our worship through faith to God, it will be heard "even afar off."

Growing in the Lord will certainly include an understanding of the necessity and blessing of making worship a central theme of our lives. Without question, God is worthy to be praised. Regardless of the circumstances of the moment, He is deserving of the highest praise at all times. This goes far beyond a mere mental acknowledgment of God and is not confined to form and ritual. True worship is the exuberant expression of a grateful soul to a gracious God. Those who choose to place worship as a priority will find that the blessings that flow back to them are multiplied many times over.

What a generous God we serve! No wonder David wrote, "One thing have I desired of the LORD, that will I seek after; that I may dwell in the house of the LORD all the days of my life, to behold the beauty of the LORD, and to enquire in his temple" (Psalm 27:4).

Test Your Knowledge

1. Define worship in your own words.
2. From the lesson, list at least three reasons why God deserves worship.

of respect for authority and an honor for those who are over us.

Certainly, the attribute of submission is needed in this present age of selfishness, pride, self-assertiveness, self-will, and "I'll do it my way" spirit. For it was just such a spirit that motivated one of God's creation to rebel. The cherub said, "I will ascend . . . I will exalt my throne . . . I will sit . . . I will be like the most High" (Isaiah 14:13-14).

This same spirit is manifested in the political, business, and social world of today and sometimes even within the church. Let us look, then, at what God's Word declares that we might value more the spirit of submission and practice it in our own lives.

Submission to God

The apostle James said, "But he giveth more grace. Wherefore he saith, God resisteth the proud, but giveth grace unto the humble. Submit yourselves therefore to God. Resist the devil, and he will flee from you" (James 4:6-7). Submission to God and His laws is necessary for angels, for mankind, and for all nature. Who can stand against the Almighty?

If we resist God, it is to our own hurt. If we oppose Him, our opposition leads to our defeat. There is no dishonor or sorrow in submitting oneself to God. True submission will lead us into His arms of safety and protection.

Note that in the passage just mentioned, James links submission with *humility:* "God resisteth the proud, but giveth grace unto the humble." Obviously, submission takes a person from the character of selfishness, self-centeredness, and self-assertion. Actually, self is the root cause of many of our troubles.

Submission to God involves *obedience*. God offers promises, not explanations. Submission will be manifested by ready obedience and yielding to God and His will.

Paul taught that in His humanity Jesus Christ, as a man, humbled Himself and obediently suffered death on the cross. (See Philippians 2:8.) His submission to the eternal plan of God required humility and obedience from His humanity. But for the joy that was set before Him He endured the cross and gave us a perfect example of submission: "Not my will but Thy will be done." (See Matthew 26:39.) He submitted His humanity to Deity.

The Spirit of God should govern our flesh and spirit. (See I Corinthians 3:9-17.) If a person will submit himself to God, then submission to the will of God and to others is not so difficult. I Corinthians 9:24-27 records, "Know ye not that they which run in a race run all, but one receiveth the prize? So run, that ye may obtain. And every man that striveth for the mastery is temperate in all things. Now they do it to obtain a corruptible crown; but we an incorruptible. I therefore so run, not as uncertainly; so fight I, not as one that beateth the air: but I keep under my body, and bring it into subjection: lest that by any means, when I have preached to others, I myself should be a castaway."

Romans 8:12-14 states it this way: "Therefore, brethren, we are debtors, not to the flesh, to live after the flesh. For if ye live after the flesh, ye shall die: but if ye through the Spirit do mortify the deeds of the body, ye shall live. For as many as are led by the Spirit of God, they are the sons of God."

The psalmist said, "Though the LORD be high, yet hath he respect unto the lowly: but the proud he knoweth afar off" (Psalm 138:6). "God resisteth the proud, but giveth grace to the humble" (James 4:6).

Submission One to Another

Every now and then we need to evaluate how we relate to other people. God so desired to relate to man in a caring, understanding manner that He purposed the Incarnation.

Having a relationship with others requires some submission on the part of both parties. Paul's epistle to the Ephesians admonished Christians to submit "yourselves one to another in the fear of God" (Ephesians 5:21).

Men and women who are filled with the Spirit are to submit to one another. In fact, the only one who can submit himself to another in the fear of Christ is the one who is filled with the Holy Ghost. The one filled with the Spirit is one who displays the fruit of the Spirit: love, joy, peace, longsuffering, gentleness, goodness, faith, meekness, and temperance. If one is full of these characteristics, he will submit himself readily.

Paul was not suggesting in Ephesians chapter 5 that we should submit to wrong teaching or doctrine. Neither was he hinting that we are to submit to inappropriate, unbiblical practices. Paul was writing to those who were in agreement concerning truth, so the assumption is that they would not be asked to submit to error.

That there is so much discord, disunity, trouble and suspicion in our world is clear evidence that many people do not obey Paul's writing. Strife leads to a spirit of faction or prejudice. Vainglory is another term for pride and conceit. But the solution to such problems is humility and personal submission to God. No person should ever be imbued with self-importance. Regardless of who we are, we need to learn to be subject to each other. The love of God shed abroad in our hearts enables us to have submission one to another.

What a fellowship when we honor and respect each other!

Husbands and Wives

The principle of submission one to another extends itself to husbands and wives. (See Ephesians 5:22-25.) Marriage is a divine institution with divine order. Paul stated, "I would have you know, that the head of every man is Christ; and the head of the woman is the man; and the head of Christ is God" (I Corinthians 11:3).

Divine order is not a subject to be taken lightly. Authority is holy and the divine order of marriage is also holy. The truth of "God as Creator" is lost when husbands and wives disregard their divinely appointed place. The consequences of such disregard are broken homes, abused women and children, and sexual deviation.

In Genesis 1:27 God was specific in making all species both male and female. When God brought the woman to the man, as recorded in Genesis 2:18-24, He established specific roles for man and woman. From the beginning the lines separating male and female were clearly defined.

Today, our world attempts to erase the differences between the sexes. This is rebellion against God's plan. When a woman wears masculine clothing, or a man puts on a woman's garment, it is an abomination to God. (See Deuteronomy 22:5.) Morever, it is serious to be an abomination in God's eyes. (See Revelation 21:27.)

Meaningful relationships do not just happen. They are a result of careful cultivation of the principles of God's Word.

Paul told husbands to love their wives. (See Ephesians 5:25-33.) This denotes a concern for their well-being, even at the expense of one's own well-being. If a husband will love his wife as Christ loves the church, the wife can safely exhibit submission to his leadership.

The apostle Paul taught that for a man to love his wife is to love himself, because he is one flesh with his wife. What he would not do to hurt himself he should not do toward his wife. A husband is ordained to protect the emotions of his wife.

So, what is the scriptural role and duty of the wife? Scripture teaches us that a woman's desire is unto her husband. (See Genesis 3:16.) This being true, a woman only hurts herself anytime she reduces the image of her husband. Nagging criticism, jealousy, self-enclosure—all of these only reduce the potential of her own growth and development. A woman needs to be loved and cherished, but she should look to and admire her husband as her head. Paul instructed the aged women to teach the young women "to love their husbands" (Titus 2:4).

A wife can build up her husband by expressing love, admiration, and respect. To challenge, embarrass, or compare him with others does not build him up; it humiliates and tears him down.

It is scriptural for a wife to be submissive, but Paul also wrote, "Submitting yourselves one to another" (Ephesians 5:21). There is to be mutual submission.

Parents and Children

If respect is going to be found anywhere in this world, it must be found at home. When respect is rooted in the home life, it will also extend beyond the walls of the home to be practiced in society.

Just as a parent wants respect, so do children. They need to be loved and given a sense of worth. Parents work hard to provide for and make better the lives of their children. However, "a man's life consisteth not in the abundance of the things which he possesseth" (Luke 12:15). Unless a child is raised to think of others and not only himself, and unless that child is taught about God, usually he will be selfish and rebellious. If everything is geared to the child's getting, comfort, and wants, then that child's concept of life is warped and distorted.

Parents are challenged to rear children who know God, who are confident, who are open and honest, who are obedient and respectful, and who are responsible and well-behaved. It is the parents' responsibility to raise, teach, and train their children in all areas of their lives—physically, morally, and spiritually. Success in this task is determined by where our real priorities are.

Authority must be administered with dignity, respect, and a sense of well-being to the child. Better children are a direct result of mother and dad being better parents. This includes sacrifice and standing for righteousness. The Word of God gives to parents endeavoring to be good parents the best possible traditions, principles, and foundation for raising children. If we neglect our children's spiritual needs, they will be raised by godless people whose life philosophies are based on human potential and not God.

To be a better parent includes the responsibility of proper parental example. Children, by nature, pattern their lifestyle after that which is around them. Hopefully, what they see is patience, honesty, nurturing, responsibility, vision, courage, and wisdom. It is vital for parents to provide the proper role models!

To be a better parent involves discipline. Dr. Grace Mitchell defines *discipline* as "the slow bit by bit time-consuming task of helping children see the sense in acting a certain way." Discipline is not always punishment. Discipline involves discipling the mind and thoughts. Resources and help in discipline can be found in the Word of God. (See Psalm 19:7-10; Proverbs 3:11-12;13:24; 22:15.)

Also, being a better parent involves exhibiting genuine love for one's children and for God! God will guide the parent when he does his best and keeps his trust and faith in God.

Children also are to respect their parents. How is it shown? *The first way respect is shown is submission and obedience.* Paul stated, "Children, obey your parents in all things: for this is well pleasing unto the Lord" (Colossians 3:20). To the church of Ephesus, the apostle stated, "Children, obey your parents in the Lord: for this is right" (Ephesians 6:1).

A second way children are to exhibit their respect for parents is by their gratitude for that which has been invested in them. The parents' sacrifices, teaching, correction, love, protection, and much more deserve gratitude and respect by the children.

Third, respect to parents can be shown by kindness. Those who fear God show kindness to others that springs forth in goodness. Kindness always multiplies itself. Kindness gives help in times of need and trouble.

Employer and Civil Authorities

Christians are also to submit themselves to their employer and to civil authority. The employee-employer relationship is suggested in Scripture by the terms servants and masters.

Paul stated, "Servants, obey in all things your masters according to the flesh; not with eyeservice, as menpleasers; but in singleness of heart, fearing God; And whatsoever ye do, do it heartily, as to the Lord, and not unto men" (Colossians 3:22-23). Peter admonished servants to "be subject to your masters with all fear; not only to the good and gentle, but also to the froward" (I Peter 2:18).

When submission is observed in the working and business world, the relationship of the employee and employer is much happier. Each party should conscientiously fulfill all the terms of the mutual working agreement.

Submission to civil authority is also important. Peter stated, "Submit yourselves to every ordinance of man for the Lord's sake: whether it be to the king, as supreme; or unto governors, as unto them that are sent by him for the punishment of evildoers, and for the praise of them that do well" (I Peter 2:13-14).

Paul the apostle wrote, "Let every soul be subject unto the higher powers. . . . Whosoever therefore resisteth the power, resisteth the ordinance of God. . . . For rulers are not a terror to good works, but to the evil . . . he is the minister of God to thee for good. . . . Wherefore ye must needs be subject . . . for conscience sake. . . . Render therefore to all their dues: tribute to whom tribute is due; custom to whom custom; fear to whom fear; honour to whom honour" (Romans 13:1-7).

As citizens, we are to submit to civil laws and authority. They are given for our well-being and protection. Should civil laws violate the Word of God, however, we should obey God. (See Acts 5:29.)

Pastoral Authority

Some Christians see pastoral authority as beneficial; some see it as binding; others simply ignore it. Regardless of one's perception, pastoral authority is crucial and beneficial for all who have submitted their lives to Jesus Christ.

God established pastoral authority to demonstrate and declare the biblical standard for God's people and to lead them into maturity and fruitfulness. God delegates the care and oversight of His people to pastors so that the people might be led, fed, taught, trained, corrected, and cared for.

The Scriptures clearly designate the purpose and the parameters of pastoral authority. (See Romans 14:1-6; Ephesians 4:15; I Thessalonians 2:11-12; 5:14; I Timothy 5:21; II Timothy 4:2; Hebrews 12:2; I Peter 5:2-3.)

In Hebrews chapter 13 the writer gave three characteristics about the relationship between a Christian and his pastor. The first is to *remember* the pastor in high esteem, honor, and respect. "Remember them which have the rule over you, who have spoken unto you the word of God: whose faith follow, considering the end of their conversation" (Hebrews 13:7).

The second admonition is to *obey* the pastor. "Obey them that have the rule over you, and submit yourselves: for they watch for your souls, as they that must give account, that they may do it with joy, and not with grief: for that is unprofitable for you" (Hebrews 13:17). It makes for a profitable growing church when one obeys the pastor who has the well-being of the flock in mind.

Third, we should *salute* the pastor. "Salute all them that have the rule over you, and all the saints" (Hebrews 13:24.) Saluting indicates submission and acknowledging authority.

Respect for Authority

"Let us hear the conclusion of the whole matter: Fear God, and keep his commandments: for this is the whole duty of man. For God shall bring every work into judgment, with every secret thing, whether it be good, or whether it be evil" (Ecclesiastes 12:13-14).

Though we are accountable, when we love and fear God, respect for authority is a delight and not a painful restraint.

Obedience and Submission

Many verses of Scripture reveal the biblical principle of obedience and submission. If we are to be saved and experience eternal life, then we should reverence God with obedience and submission.

Paul said, "I speak after the manner of men because of the infirmity of your flesh: for as ye have yielded your members servants to uncleanness and to iniquity unto iniquity; even so now yield your members servants to righteousness unto holiness. . . . But now being made free from sin, and become servants to God, ye have your fruit unto holiness, and the end everlasting life" (Romans 6:19, 22).

A person must yield to righteousness if he is to experience it. Righteousness involves making the right decisions and avoiding the wrong ones. Righteousness precedes holiness and holiness precedes everlasting life, but it all begins with yielding one's spirit to God in submission and obedience.

Jesus' prayed, "Not my will be done, but thine be done." He was obedient even unto death—the most vile death possible—on a cross. (See Philippians 2:8.)

In order for one to truly learn obedience and submission, suffering is involved. As Jesus exemplified when He was obedient unto the death of the cross, so we should willingly submit ourselves to Him. It is suffering that touches self. Satan knew this when he asked God to take away the hedge from around Job. (See Job 1:10-11.)

Some can obey God day and night until their patience is tried or suffering is involved. Many try to pick and choose their own way, but obedience and submission is really not learned until one can be a servant even in the time of suffering.

Life puts us to the test and tries our love and faith for God. Through every test we prove the genuineness of these attributes in our lives.

Peter said to Jesus, "I will not deny thee." (See Matthew 26:35.) But what a change is evident in Peter as he weeps bitterly the following morning. Suffering makes a man see whether he really is all that he thinks he is. And, consequently, perfect submission never comes until we have passed through suffering.

Test Your Knowledge

1. Define submission.
2. Submission is linked with what two characteristics?
3. What are some causes of discord, disunity, and trouble?
4. What is a key responsibility of the husband?
5. What are some needs of children today?
6. How can one show respect to parents?
7. In what three ways can a Christian have a better relationship with his pastor?

Apply Your Knowledge

After reading this chapter and praying for a spirit of submission, determine to be a better companion, parent, worker, Christian, and citizen. Jesus said, "Whosoever will save his life shall lose it: and whosoever will lose his life for my sake shall find it" (Matthew 16:25).

Expand Your Knowledge

Besides the many books that are written by Pentecostal authors on this subject, one may wish to further his study with authors such as Fritz Ridenour, John Benton, James Dobson, and Charles Swindoll.

8 Loving God and Our Neighbor

And thou shalt love the LORD thy God with all thine heart, and with all thy soul, and with all thy might.

Deuteronomy 6:5

Start with the Scriptures

Luke 10:30-37   I John 2:8
John 13:34-35   II John 5
Ephesians 5:29

According to Jewish rabbinic teachings, the law of Moses consists of 613 commandments regulating virtually every aspect of life in ancient Israel. Though the Ten Commandments are certainly notable among the 613, they are nevertheless only ten commandments among many.

As if these 613 were not enough, there arose in Jewish tradition many more commandments, the oral law, which God had allegedly given to Moses on Mount Sinai in addition to the written law. At the time Jesus walked on this earth, this oral law, or Talmud, was not yet written down. The writing of these traditional sayings took place about A.D. 200.

Jesus did not have the same appreciation for the oral law as did the religious leaders of Israel in the first century. He refused to recognize it as being authoritative; indeed, He seemed to intentionally flaunt His disregard for these traditions. For example, when Jesus healed a blind man on the Sabbath day, He spat on the ground, made clay with the saliva, anointed the eyes of the blind man with the clay, and said to the blind man, "Go, wash in the pool of Siloam" (John 9:7).

According to the Jewish Talmud, on the Sabbath day one may spit on a rock, but he may not spit on the ground. The reason for this is that spitting on a rock produces nothing, whereas spitting on the ground makes mud, and that is work. But Jesus not only spat on the ground, He also intentionally made clay on the Sabbath. As if that were not enough, Jesus anointed the eyes of the blind man with the clay. Jewish tradition prohibited touching a blind man; he was considered unclean. It also prohibited coming into contact with another person's saliva; that was considered unclean. Thus on several points, Jesus knowingly and intentionally violated the Jewish oral law.

After this, Jesus commanded the blind man to go and wash in the pool of Siloam. This pool of water was located at the extreme southern edge of the city of Jerusalem. Though we cannot be certain, it is reasonable to assume that from where Jesus and the blind man stood when He commanded the man to go and wash to the pool of Siloam exceeded a Sabbath day's journey. Jewish tradition limited travel on the Sabbath day to about 3,000 to 3,600 feet. There are many places in Jerusalem more than this distance from the pool of Siloam.

Jesus declared that the worship of the scribes and Pharisees was in vain, for they taught "as doctrines the commandments of men" (Matthew 15:9). The law of Moses itself prohibited the addition of any commandments to the written revelation. (See Deuteronomy 4:2.) But ostensibly to help them avoid the transgression of God's commandments, the ancient Jews added many commandments of man. Their intention was to build a "fence" around the law. (See Aboth 1:1 in the Mishnah.) Jesus was unhappy with this fence because, as human commandments always will, they became even more important to the Jews than the commandments of God Himself. Later, Paul would join his voice with that of Jesus in condemning the doctrines and commandments of men. (See Colossians 2:20-23.)

According to Jesus, only the commandments of God were of any significance. And, when asked to identify which was the greatest of the 613 commandments of the law, He immediately responded: "The first of all the commandments is, Hear, O Israel; the Lord our God is one Lord: And thou shalt love the Lord thy God with all thy heart, and with all thy soul, and with all thy mind, and with all thy strength: this is the first commandment. And the second is like, namely this, Thou shalt love thy neighbour as thyself. There is none other commandment greater than these" (Mark 12:29-31). (See also Matthew 22:34-40.)

It is fascinating that neither of the commandments Jesus identified as first and second in significance among the 613 commandments are included in the Ten Commandments. The first is found in Deuteronomy 6:4-5; the second is from Leviticus 19:18.

The First Commandment

The commandment identified by Jesus as the first of all is known among the Jewish people as the

Shema. Shema means "hear," and it is the first word in Deuteronomy 6:4. The first word of the commandment thus became shorthand to represent the entire command.

Jewish scribes copying the Hebrew Scriptures use an interesting typographical technique to focus the attention of the reader on Deuteronomy 6:4. On the page in the Hebrew Bible where the verse appears, the last letter of the first word and the last letter of the last word of the *Shema* are written oversized. The same is true in the printed Hebrew text. To the eye accustomed to reading the Hebrew language, this has the same effect as underlining or highlighting the text.

Obviously, the non-Messianic Jewish authorities who preserve the Hebrew text do not give Deuteronomy 6:4 this special attention because of what Jesus said. They do this because it is universally recognized among Jews that the *Shema* is the pivotal text of the Hebrew Scriptures. The words of the *Shema* are the first on the lips of an Orthodox Jewish person when he awakens in the morning, and the last before he falls asleep at night. Several times throughout the day, he will recite the *Shema*. They are the last words he speaks before dying.

It is because of the radical monotheism of the *Shema* that the Jewish people refuse to embrace any form of polytheism. Yahweh (Jehovah) their Elohim (God) is *one*. They are right to reject any theology that compromises the oneness of God.

But the *Shema* does not stop with the declaration of God's oneness; it continues with the admonition to love Him with all one's heart, soul, and strength. According to Mark, Jesus quoted the *Shema* as, "Hear, O Israel; The Lord our God is one Lord: And thou shalt love the Lord thy God with all thy heart, and with all thy soul, and with all thy mind, and with all thy strength" (Mark 12:29-30). Jesus expanded the *Shema* to include loving God with the mind.

With our Western mindset, which is heavily influenced by Greek philosophy, we tend to view each aspect of man separately. That is, the heart is one thing, the soul another, the mind another, and the strength another. But the ancient Hebrews viewed man as a unified being; man was seen as an integrated whole, not as fragmented into separate parts.

The Hebrews were a visceral people; mental activity and emotions were tied to the inner organs of the body. The Hebrew word translated "reins" in the KJV means "kidneys." (See Job 16:13; 19:27; Psalm 7:9; 16:7; 26:2; 73:21; 139:13; Proverbs 23:16; Isaiah 11:5; Jeremiah 11:20; 12:2; 17:10; 20:12; Lamentations 3:13.) In Jewish thought, the kidneys were the seat of the character, affections, and emotions. The liver was identified with anger. (See Lamentations 2:11.) The heart was equated with the will. (See Deuteronomy 6:5; Psalm 119:2; Proverbs 3:5; Ecclesiastes 8:11.) This is seen in the New Testament in such phrases as "bowels of compassion" (I John 3:17). The Greek word *splangchna*, translated "bowels" in the KJV, is accurately translated; it means "intestines."

All of this illustrates that to the Jews, there was no mind/body split. Western anthropology on the verge of the twenty-first century is strongly influenced by Greek philosophy; the body tends to be viewed as evil, and man is considered to be a spirit imprisoned in a body. But Jewish anthropology views man as a whole. For example, though Adam's body was formed of the dust of the ground, as God breathed the breath of life into his nostrils, he became "a living soul" (Genesis 2:7). When the God of Israel declares "all souls are mine" (Ezekiel 18:4), He does not mean just that the immaterial part of man belongs to Him, but that man in his totality—all that makes man, man—belongs to Him. Eight souls were saved in Noah's ark; this means, of course, eight people (I Peter 3:20).

There certainly are material and immaterial components to man's existence (Hebrews 4:12; I Thessalonians 5:23), but from the perspective of the Hebrews, to speak of any component was to address the whole of man. This does not mean that the Hebrews were unaware of the distinction between the material and immaterial components of human existence, but that they tended to think of human existence in a holistic way.

When Abraham asked Sarah to say she was his sister, he explained he wished her to do this so his "soul" could live (Genesis 12:13). The NKJV rightly translates this, "That I may live." Throughout the Hebrew Scriptures, "soul" is used as a metaphor for "person." (See, for example, Exodus 12:15, 19; 31:14; Leviticus 4:2; 5:1, 2, 4) The Hebrew Scriptures frequently use "body" to refer to the material part of a man who is dead (e.g., Leviticus 21:11), or to refer to one's reproductive abilities (e.g., Deuteronomy 28:4), but when referring to a living person, virtually any part of human existence represented the whole.

An example of this is seen in the New Testament by comparing Mark 8:36 with Luke 9:25. Mark is written by a Jewish author accustomed to viewing human nature in a holistic way, and he reports Jesus saying, "For what shall it profit a man, if he shall gain the whole world, and lose his own soul?" Luke, however, was a Gentile writing to a Gentile audience, and he records Jesus saying, "For what is a man advantaged, if he gain the whole world, and lose himself, or be cast away?" Mark understood losing one's soul as losing one's self, not as merely losing one's immaterial part. Luke, aware of the influence of Greek philosophy and its tendency to fragment man into the material and immaterial parts, did not use the word "soul," for that could have been understood to refer merely to the immaterial part. Instead, he reported the *meaning* of Jesus' words: Jesus warned against the loss of one's self.

The significance of all this for the *Shema* is this: Moses' point was not to fragment humanity into separate components of the heart, the soul, strength, or—as reported by Jesus according to Mark—the mind. What Moses meant was that human beings are to love God with all that they are; they are to love Him holistically. (The word "holistic" comes from the Greek *holos*, which is used three times in the Septuagint translation of Deuteronomy 6:5, explaining how "wholly" God is to be loved. *Holos* means "whole, entire, complete.") Thus, one cannot genuinely love God with the heart without loving Him with one's strength. One cannot love God with the soul without loving Him with the mind. The words "heart," "soul," and so forth are used to point out that no part of man's existence is exempt from the requirement to love God.

It is also helpful to note that the biblical Hebrew vocabulary had only words for "love" and "hate." There was no word to express fondness, or to express the idea of liking someone or something short of love. In other words, there were no words in the Hebrew vocabulary to express degrees of love or of hatred. This does not mean that the Hebrews themselves were incapable of experiencing degrees of love and hatred; their vocabulary was simply limited.

Anything less than complete and devout love was considered hatred, so the idea of hatred had to carry the broad range of semantic meaning included in many English words today. This helps us understand Jesus' warning to the person who did not hate "his father, and mother, and wife, and children, and brethren, and sisters, yea, and his own life also." To hate these is a condition for being Jesus' disciple. (See Luke 14:26.) But the New Testament elsewhere urges believers to love the same people Jesus said we must hate. (See Ephesians 5:25-33; 6:1-4; Colossians 3:19-21.) The puzzle is solved when we recognize the meaning of "love" and "hate" to the Hebrew mind. What Jesus meant was that our love for God must be preeminent; in comparison, our love for others falls into the semantic range of meaning expressed by the word "hate." It would perhaps help us understand this if we substituted the words "love less" for the word "hate."

So when the *Shema* says we are to love God with all our heart, soul, mind, and strength, it means we are to be completely, fully, unreservedly devoted to Him with all we are, to such a degree that our devotion to anyone else seems by comparison to be hatred. We are to put our complete entities into His service, including both our material and immaterial parts. Paul had this same idea in mind when he wrote: "I beseech you therefore, brethren, by the mercies of God, that ye present your bodies a living sacrifice, holy, acceptable unto God, which is your reasonable service. And be not conformed to this world: but be ye transformed by the renewing of your mind, that ye may prove what is that good, and acceptable, and perfect, will of God" (Romans 12:1-2).

The Second Commandment

According to Jesus, the second commandment is similar to the first: "And the second is like, namely this, Thou shalt love thy neighbour as thyself. There is none other commandment greater than these" (Mark 12:31).

To Jesus, pure religion was not simply emotional attachments either to God or to others. Just as believers are to love God not only with their immaterial part, but also with their material, including their very strength, so we are to love our neighbors. That is, we are to involve ourselves in relationships with others that demonstrate love in practical ways.

When a lawyer asked Jesus what he should do to inherit eternal life, Jesus asked him, "What is written in the law? how readest thou?" (Luke 10:26). The lawyer answered, "Thou shalt love the Lord thy God with all thy heart, and with all thy soul, and with all thy strength, and with all thy mind; and thy neighbour as thyself" (Luke 10:27). Jesus responded, "Thou hast answered right: this do, and thou shalt live" (Luke 10:28). But the lawyer wanted to justify himself, so he asked Jesus, "And who is my neighbour?" (Luke 10:29). It is at this point that Jesus told the parable of the Good Samaritan. (See Luke 10:30-37.)

Jesus' point was that strict adherence to the law of Moses prevented people from demonstrating love and compassion to the hurting. Even the lawyer questioning Jesus had asked the question "Who is my neighbour?" because he wanted to justify himself. But when Jesus asked, "Which now of these three, thinkest thou, was neighbour unto him that fell among the thieves?" (Luke 10:36), the lawyer was compelled to answer, "He that shewed mercy on him" (Luke 10:37). Apparently, the lawyer could not bring himself to say, "The Samaritan." The idea that the law limited love, and that a Samaritan could be an example for Jews to follow, shocked this lawyer. Jesus put the entire meaning of the command to love one's neighbor into perspective when He said, "Go, and do thou likewise" (Luke 10:37).

There is nothing esoteric to the second greatest commandment; it simply means we must look for and act upon opportunities to help those who are hurting. This is what James had in mind when he wrote, "Pure religion and undefiled before God and the Father is this, To visit the fatherless and widows in their affliction, and to keep himself unspotted from the world" (James 1:27).

The Law and the Prophets

In Matthew's account of Jesus' identification of the two great commandments, he records Jesus as saying, "On these two commandments hang all the law and the prophets" (Matthew 22:40). The word translated "hang" has to do with driving a peg or nail in a wall to support clothing or whatever may be hung on it. Jesus' point is that the entire Hebrew Scriptures "hang" on the concept of loving God and loving others. All the Old Testament is written to bring men to love God and others. Every commandment in the Hebrew Scriptures is intended in some way to promote the love of God or the love of people.

Indeed, even the Ten Commandments are structured in this way. The first four gave Israel the ways they were to love God; the last six gave them the ways they were to love others. In order to love God, they were not to have any other gods before Him; they were not to make and worship carved images; they were not to take His name in vain; they were to keep the Sabbath holy. In order to love others, they were to honor their parents, to refrain from murder, from adultery, from stealing, from bearing false witness against their neighbors, and from coveting that which was their neighbor's. (See Exodus 20:1-17.)

All the rest of the 613 commandments in the law of Moses can also be put in one of the two categories: they promote love either for God or for others.

The New Commandment

It is no surprise, then, that Jesus said, "A new commandment I give unto you, That ye love one another; as I have loved you, that ye also love one another. By this shall all men know that ye are my disciples, if ye have love one to another" (John 13:34-35). John, who recorded this commandment, later wrote, "He that saith he is in the light, and hateth his brother, is in darkness even until now. He that loveth his brother abideth in the light, and there is none occasion of stumbling in him. But he that hateth his brother is in darkness, and walketh in darkness, and knoweth not whither he goeth, because that darkness hath blinded his eyes" (I John 2:9-11). This, according to John, is the new commandment. (See I John 2:8.) John refers to this commandment again in his second letter: "And now I beseech thee . . . not as though I wrote a new commandment unto thee, but that which we have had from the beginning, that we love one another" (II John 5).

This commandment was not new with John; it had been given by Jesus "from the beginning." It is what summarized Jesus' message as it related to the believer's relationship with others.

It is said that Rabbi Hillel, a contemporary of Jesus, was asked by a skeptical student to explain the whole law while the student stood on one foot. Hillel answered, "Whatever is hateful to you, do not to another." This, according to Hillel, summed up the teaching of the Hebrew Scriptures.

Jesus, answering a similar question, declared that the two greatest commandments of the law were to love God and to love other people. These two, He said, sum up all the Old Testament has to say.

Jesus was not impressed with the commandments and traditions of men expressed in the oral law. He rebuked the Pharisees for the proliferation of human commandments, declaring that these traditions prevented them from obeying the commandments of God. Repeatedly, in His parables and by His actions, He demonstrated the tendency of legalism to prevent people from reaching out to help the hurting. As far as He was concerned, the greatest good was for a man to love God with all his being. The next greatest was for a man to love others—in practical ways—as he loves himself.

Test Your Knowledge

1. How many commandments are included in the law of Moses?

2. What is the meaning of the word *Shema*?

3. Explain the Hebrew view of the relationship between the material and immaterial parts of man.

4. Discuss the meaning of the Hebrew words for "love" and "hate."

5. How does one demonstrate his love for God? for others?

6. Why did the priest and the Levite pass by the wounded man in the parable of the Good Samaritan?

7. Why did Jesus use a Samaritan as the hero in the parable?

Apply Your Knowledge

Perhaps you know someone who is hurting in some way. Is he depressed? physically sick? emotionally wounded? What can you do to help him? This week do at least two specific things to reach out to someone in pain. Perhaps you can send a card, make a phone call, or even pay a personal visit. Report the results to your class next week.

Expand Your Knowledge

Read through the Gospel of John this week and list all the ways Jesus showed His disregard for the Jewish traditions.

At your local library, you should be able to check out a copy of the *Mishnah*, a portion of the Jewish oral tradition. Scan this book and familiarize yourself with the kinds of human commandments which arose around the law of Moses and served to choke out the true significance of the law's emphasis on loving God and loving others.

9 Humility Personified

Humble yourselves in the sight of the Lord, and he shall lift you up.

James 4:10

Start with the Scriptures

Luke 14:11; 18:9-14
Philippians 2:1-11
I Peter 5:5

What royal prerogatives Christ might have claimed had He wished! What irrefutable rights!

The Lord might have come to this earth in magnificent splendor. He might have made much of the fact that angels were in His attendance. He could have come in princely robes. He might have demanded worship from the smallest to the greatest. He could have provided signs and miracles to His Jewish enemies when they requested it.

Jesus Christ could have done these things and so

much more. Instead, the Lord came to this earth without honors. He intentionally laid aside any rank or privilege that might have won the fickle favor of the world. In a magnificent display of love and humility Christ came. He came down from the portals of glory in order to reach man in his darkness and sin.

Empty of Self, Full of God

Our society teaches us by example to grasp for every bit of glory we can obtain. Some people pay a high price for the applause of the crowd. Others compromise their morals and convictions for a brief moment of political or social fame.

How exceptional, then, to read that Christ "made himself of no reputation" (Philippians 2:7). He who was essentially one with God "did not think this equality with God was a thing to be eagerly grasped or retained" (Philippians 2:6, *The Amplified Bible*).

Was Jesus Christ really God in flesh? He certainly was, but in His earthly ministry He did not tenaciously hold on to that distinction. In fact, the phrase "made himself of no reputation" means that He emptied Himself of all the privileges that were rightfully His.

Very few strip themselves of privileges in these days. Very few are living the crucified life. It costs so much to esteem others better than ourselves. (See Philippians 2:3.) It is so hard on natural pride to let others step ahead of us.

Still this was the very principle that the apostle Paul was teaching believers when he wrote, "Let this mind be in you, which was also in Christ Jesus" (Philippians 2:5). *The Amplified Bible* reads, "Let Him be your example in humility."

The Lord humbled Himself. No one could have snatched away the splendor that appropriately belonged to Christ. But He could and did submit Himself to abuse and mistreatment. The submission of the man Jesus was the very thing that the Father desired of His Son. (See John 8:29.)

Paul noted the deep descent taken by Christ in His self-humiliation. The Lord "made himself of no reputation, and took upon him the form of a servant, and was made in the likeness of men: And being found in fashion as a man, he humbled himself, and became obedient unto death, even the death of the cross" (Philippians 2:7-8).

In God's plan humiliation always comes before exaltation. The lowly road that Christ followed led from one painful experience to another until He was finally glorified. Forever concerned about others, He was always being misunderstood, or reviled, or spat upon. But He was willing to walk in God's perfecting way. "Though he were a Son, yet learned he obedience by the things which he suffered" (Hebrews 5:8).

Because of Christ's obedience "God also hath highly exalted him, and given him a name which is above every name" (Philippians 2:9). Men slandered Him and crucified Him, but God exalted Him. His name, once rejected, has been placed high above all others. No wonder a favorite, old hymn states,

"At the name of Jesus bowing,
Falling prostrate at His feet,
King of kings in heav'n we'll crown Him,
When our journey is complete."

Through the Back Door

Christ could have come to this world through the front door of fame and privilege. Instead, He came quietly through the back door. He came through the servants' quarters.

While some are born in stately mansions or magnificent palaces, the Lord Jesus was born on the backstage of history. His cradle was a manger (perhaps an open box of a stable where livestock found fodder). There was nothing glamorous there. His whole life would be marked by poverty. He told a potential follower that the Son of man had nowhere to lay His head. "Though he was rich, yet for your sakes he became poor, that ye through his poverty might be rich" (II Corinthians 8:9).

At the Last Supper, while His disciples quarreled with one another over "which of them should be accounted the greatest" (Luke 22:24), the Lord poured water in a basin to wash their feet. "I am," He told them, "among you as he that serveth" (Luke 22:27).

The apostle Paul was astonished, not only that Christ died, but that He died the ignominious death of the cross. To be crucified was the ultimate step which the Savior could have taken. It led Him to the utmost humility and shame. He became a curse for others by hanging on a tree. (See Galatians 3:13.) No wonder Christ struggled so hard in Gethsemane. No wonder He threw Himself on the ground and prayed so desperately. No wonder the sweat on His troubled brow was as great drops of blood. There, in the garden, He foresaw the overwhelming disgrace and degradation of Calvary. But, as Paul declared, "He humbled himself, and became obedient unto death, even the death of the cross" (Philippians 2:8).

The Role of a Servant

Such was the love of Jesus Christ. He might have highly exalted Himself as the Messiah, but instead He laid aside His majesty "so as to assume the guise of a servant" (Philippians 2:7, *The Amplified Bible*). Compassionately He performed His humble role, and even the most lowly were ministered to. Meanwhile His true identity went undetected by those haughty rulers in Judea, "for had they known it, they would not have crucified the Lord of glory" (I Corinthians 2:8). What a mistake they made! Here was the Sovereign of the universe opening the eyes of blind beggars and healing the wounds of poor lepers, and the authorities, in their arrogance, condemned Him.

Despite Christ's own efforts to find seclusion and avoid public acclaim, the Bible says, "He could not be hid" (Mark 7:24). People were constantly pressing Him with genuine needs and selfish ambitions. Even the disciples misunderstood that His greatest mission was one of service and sacrifice.

During Christ's last journey to Jerusalem, James and John came with their mother to ask a request of the Master. The two men simply wanted, so they told Jesus, to "sit, the one on thy right hand, and the other on the left, in thy kingdom" (Matthew 20:21). The sons of Zebedee had completely bypassed the true character of Christ's kingdom, so Jesus taught His disciples that there would be a new type of relationship among His subjects. "Whosoever will be great among you, let him be your minister; and whosoever will be chief among you, let him be your servant: even as the Son of man came not to be ministered unto, but to minister, and to give his life a ransom for many" (Matthew 20:26-28).

A Tale of Two Sinners

There was little need for the Lord to give a definition of religious pride while He was teaching the Jewish people. There standing before Him on a daily basis were the self-important Pharisees. Many of their lives perfectly illustrated the conceit that ran counter to Christ's gospel message.

Eloquently the Lord drew a picture of two men, one a Pharisee and the other a publican. Both had gone to the Temple to pray, but beyond that fact there seemed to be little similarity between the two. Their individual approach to God was entirely different, as was their motive for praying.

The Pharisee's prayer began by acknowledging his superiority over others. "God, I thank thee, that I am not as other men are, extortioners, unjust, adulterers, or even as this publican" (Luke 18:11). This shameful comparison was quickly followed by the Pharisee's brazen reminder to God of how religiously he had fasted and paid tithes.

The tax collector, standing afar off, felt corrupted by his own transgressions. His head bowed, the publican smote his breast and humbly asked, "God be merciful to me a sinner" (Luke 18:13). No pretentious words here. No claim to special privileges from God. Just a desperate plea that he might somehow be forgiven of his sins.

Obviously both men went up to the Temple as sinners, but only one was justified. The difference was simply in their attitudes. The publican knew he was a sinner and repented; the Pharisee acknowledged only the sins of others and displeased God. Then, lest we should miss the message, Jesus declared, "For every one that exalteth himself shall be abased; and he that humbleth himself shall be exalted" (Luke 18:14).

It may seem a paradox, but for the Christian the way up is down; the route to receiving comes through giving; the road to life is through death.

When You Lose Your Way

The young man wept. He wept unashamedly after he had stood to his feet in church to testify of how God had changed his life. He explained that his ways had been very wicked but that the Lord had been very patient. One day, as a new convert, he had been taken off guard. He had actually taken the name of the Lord in vain in the dairy where he worked. But quickly the young man had fallen on his knees to ask forgiveness. Even then God was waiting and restored the young man's hope.

Humility is an accurate evaluation of who we really are. It acknowledges the greatness of the Lord. It stands back in awe of all God's magnificent holiness and His abundant mercy.

At times we may all get a little confused, especially if we have been mistreated or misjudged. We may well have experienced something that is unfair. The natural tendency at this moment is to lash back, to defend ourselves, to justify our cause, to give someone "a piece of our mind."

In just such a situation we have a golden opportunity to manifest a Christ-like spirit. Diamonds are fashioned under intense pressure, and likewise, the fruit of the Spirit is best produced during crisis. If we choose the humble way, the way that Jesus took, we will certainly gain God's favor as well as man's.

Christ sacrificed His own needs for those of the thronging multitudes. He went beyond the second and third mile for you and me who were strangers. He took the attitude that everyone in need is a neighbor. Even on the cross the Lord manifested this spirit as He prayed, not for Himself, but for His enemies.

The lowly, humble road of servanthood and humility is not the road most traveled, but it is the route that Jesus took, and it leads to tremendous blessing.

What Jesus Saw

Some people are always looking for the grand and glorious. They crave the spectacular. Like the Pharisees of old, they want to be seen of men, to be applauded, to be praised. They use subtle methods to draw attention to themselves, and then they feign a humility that is anything but genuine.

Jesus noticed the humble services of others along His way. At a Pharisee's supper He carefully observed a sinner woman who meekly began to wash His feet. Her tears were precious to the Master for they spoke of her deep sense of guilt and remorse. To the self-righteous Pharisees, the woman was untouchable; to Jesus her touch was commendable.

While they criticized, she worshiped. And so, as Christ reproved His haughty host, He approved the humble woman: "Seest thou this woman? I entered into thine house, thou gavest me no water for my feet: but she hath washed my feet with tears, and wiped them with the hairs of her head. Thou gavest me no kiss: but this woman since the time I came in hath not ceased to kiss my feet. My head with oil thou didst not anoint: but this woman hath anointed my feet with ointment. Wherefore I say unto thee, Her sins, which are many, are forgiven; for she loved much: but to whom little is forgiven, the same loveth little" (Luke 7:44-47).

It was marvelous what Jesus saw. One day as He sat down opposite the treasury, Christ "beheld how the people cast money into the treasury: and many that were rich cast in much" (Mark 12:41). What really captured the Lord's attention, however, was a poverty-stricken widow. Her donation was only two copper mites, the least of Jewish coins. But Jesus emphasized to the disciples that she had put in more than all those giving to the treasury. "For all they did cast in of their abundance; but she of her want did cast in all she had, even all her living" (Mark 12:44).

On the Anvil

They came from various backgrounds and with an assortment of abilities. Yet all the people who were greatly used by God seemed to share one thing in common: they all learned the lesson of submission. Often it was a costly lesson, learned on the steel-faced anvil of God. Within His workshop they were cast into shape by the heavy hand of circumstance. The heat was intense, the blows severe. Gradually, however, their lives took on a form that was pleasing to the Master.

Did you hear those ringing blows as the great smith's hammer struck against white-hot iron? That was Moses being shaped in the image of the One who was to come. The similarities between Moses, Israel's deliverer, and Christ were striking. Moses himself declared, "The LORD thy God will raise up unto thee a Prophet from the midst of thee, of thy brethren, like unto me; unto him ye shall hearken" (Deuteronomy 18:15).

The Scriptures tell us that "the man Moses was very meek, above all the men which were upon the face of the earth" (Numbers 12:3). Like Christ, he learned obedience by the things that he suffered. Someone has said that Moses spent forty years thinking he was something, forty years learning he was nothing, and forty years learning what God could do with nothing. While it was the Lord Himself who drew Israel "out of the iron furnace, even out of Egypt" (Deuteronomy 4:20), it was Moses who became His special instrument of liberation.

Another of those humble instruments that the Lord fashioned was a woman called Esther. Eventually, through the providence of God, she became queen of Persia, but before that she was only Hadassah, a Jewish orphan girl. Trained by Mordecai, her foster parent, Esther showed remarkable courage and wisdom. In the face of a royal decree (which obviously could not be altered) she stood true and saved her people from extermination.

Fiery trials in the lives of the righteous are not unusual. (See I Peter 4:12). The Scriptures tell us that Joseph "was sold for a servant: whose feet they hurt with fetters: he was laid in iron" (Psalm 105:17-18). The iron indeed entered his soul. The wicked betrayal of his brothers, the false accusations of those whom he faithfully served, and the extended time he spent in prison might easily have made him bitter. Instead Joseph became better—a better son, a better administrator, and, most importantly, a better type of Jesus Christ.

The Problem with Pride

God looks beyond our actions and judges our attitudes. The divine perspective is far more penetrating than the human. "All the ways of a man are clean in his own eyes; but the LORD weigheth the spirits" (Proverbs 16:2).

God sees pride as a treacherous monster that leads its victim to a terrible fall. Pride was the downfall of Lucifer and destroyed men of renown such as Ahithophel, Uzziah, and Haman. Somehow it blinds its prey to reality, and while others may sense what is coming, the proud push arrogantly onward. Pride is the height of self-deception and ignorance. (See Galatians 6:3; I Timothy 6:4.)

All the good advice of concerned pastors, loving relatives, and Christian friends often goes unheeded by the proud. The proud are enormously conceited. Once they have made their plans, there is no turning back. The price of retreat seems worse to them than any possible consequence.

The humble child of God, in contrast, is teachable. When he fails he wants to be corrected. In fact, the spiritual person welcomes instruction: "Reprove not a scorner, lest he hate thee: rebuke a wise man, and he will love thee" (Proverbs 9:8).

What a difference our attitude makes! Constantly the Scriptures present us with two options concerning our behavior: one is to act upon pride, and the other is to behave with humility. The contrast is pronounced. The two ways have extremely different results. God Himself has emphasized, through His Word, the importance of making the right choice: "Though the LORD be high, yet hath he respect unto the lowly: but the proud he knoweth afar off" (Psalm 138:6).

Test Your Knowledge

1. How can we have the mind of Christ?
2. How did Jesus take on the form of a servant?
3. What was so humiliating about the death of the cross?
4. In Luke 18:9-14 how did the publican find justification?
5. What is humility?
6. Give two examples from the New Testament of humble service toward Christ.
7. Who were some of those humble instruments that God used in the Old Testament?
8. What are some of the characteristics of the proud?

Apply Your Knowledge

Have you had personal experiences where you have allowed pride to dominate your thinking? What were some of the consequences?

Consider some of the times when you have taken a humble position. How did this affect your walk with God?

Expand Your Knowledge

The next chapter deals with living faith. Decide how humility and faith are related. What humble steps were taken by the faith-filled individuals of Hebrews chapter 11?

Living Faith

So then faith cometh by hearing, and hearing by the word of God.

Romans 10:17

Start with the Scriptures

Romans 10:17   Hebrews 11:1-12
II Thessalonians 3:2   James 2:20, 22, 26

There are three qualities by which Paul assessed the relative maturity and spirituality of the churches to which he wrote. These qualities are faith, hope, and love. In general, Paul commended each church in the early verses of his letters for one or more of these qualities. If any one of the three is missing in his commendation, it seems the letter is written to deal with the quality or qualities in which the church is deficient.

In Romans 1:8, Paul commended the church at

Rome for its faith, which was so well known as to be the topic of discussion among believers everywhere. Again in verse 12, he commended the Romans for this quality. Although hope is mentioned ten times in the letter, in no case is the church at Rome commended for its hope. Instead, Paul prays that they will abound in hope (Romans 15:13). Love is mentioned eleven times in the letter, but as with hope, there is no commendation for the Romans' love. There are, however, repeated encouragements to love (Romans 8:28; 12:9-10; 13:8-10).

The church at Corinth was a carnal church (I Corinthians 3:1), and Paul did not commend them for faith, hope, or love. Instead, he identified all three qualities as suitable goals for the Corinthians to reach for (I Corinthians 13:13). The church at Corinth apparently matured in the quality of faith by the time Paul wrote his second letter to them (II Corinthians 1:24; 10:15). Although they had matured in love as well, Paul asked them to prove the sincerity of their love (II Corinthians 8:7-8, 24).

The churches of Galatia were being swayed from their exclusive faith in Jesus Christ to a form of Judaism (Galatians 1:6-9). It is no surprise, then, that Paul did not commend them for faith, hope, or love. Instead, he encouraged them to develop these qualities. His encouragement to develop faith is seen in Galatians 3:2, 5, 7-9, 11, 14, 23-26; 5:5-6, 22. He encouraged them to develop hope in Galatians 5:5. Encouragement to develop love is seen in Galatians 5:6, 13-14, 22.

The church in Ephesus was a relatively mature church, and Paul commended the believers there for their faith and love (Ephesians 1:15). Since they were apparently deficient in hope, Paul prayed that they would grow in that area (Ephesians 1:18). It is discovered in Revelation 2:4, however, that by the time John wrote the final book in the New

Testament, the Ephesian church had turned away from the love they once had.

Paul commended the Philippians for their faith (Philippians 1:25; 2:17) and prayed that their love would abound more (Philippians 1:9). Though they apparently had a measure of love, it needed to develop and mature (Philippians 2:2). He did not commend them for their hope.

Paul commended the Colossians for their faith, hope, and love (Colossians 1:4-5). The essential message of the book is that the believers should stand fast in their relationship with Jesus Christ and not be moved by legalists, mystics, or ascetics.

One of the most interesting examples of the way in which faith, hope, and love are Paul's yardsticks to measure the maturity and spiritual well-being of a church is seen in his letters to the Thessalonians. In his first letter, he commended the believers for their faith, hope, and love (I Thessalonians 1:3). But after he wrote his first letter, some false teacher had apparently forged a letter under Paul's name to the Thessalonians claiming that the day of Christ had already come (II Thessalonians 2:1-2). This false teaching robbed the Thessalonians of their hope, so Paul could commend them only for their faith and love (II Thessalonians 1:3). Clearly, Paul's second letter was written to restore hope to the Thessalonians (II Thessalonians 2:3-17).

Like most of the first century churches, the church at Rome needed to mature in areas related to the biblical measurement of maturity and spirituality. Specifically, the believers in Rome were deficient in hope and love.

Paul's common pattern in his letters to churches was to commend them for whatever strength he could identify in the early verses, then to correct whatever deficiencies or excesses he saw in the main body of the letter, and finally to commend them again for their strengths in the closing verses. His final commendation to the Romans comes in Romans 16:19. This has been called Paul's "plus-minus-plus" or "positive-negative-positive" technique. When it is necessary to offer correction, it is wise first to commend and to reinforce the commendation after the correction has been given. This principle is useful in all relationships, including the parent-child relationship. It is wise for spiritual leaders to use this approach in preaching, teaching, and counseling.

Since faith is one of the three qualities that endure (I Corinthians 13:13) and thus one of the measurements of Christian maturity, we must discover what faith is, how it is obtained, and how to live by faith. (See II Corinthians 5:7.)

What Faith Is

The word "faith," or some form of it, is used well over 200 times in the New Testament, but there is much confusion as to what faith is.

Words alone are not the realities they represent. Words are merely codes to describe something else, whether imagined or real. For example, the word "chair" is not a chair. It is a code which represents the idea of a chair to the mind. It is impossible to sit down on the word "chair."

When it comes to faith, it is not all in *saying*, "I believe." It is in the *actual believing* and in having the right object of our belief.

As is always the case, when error is embraced, the result is confusion, which brings condemnation, frustration, and a sense of hopelessness. It even causes some people to question God.

Because of a failure to understand the essence of faith, many good people struggle "trying to believe," saying, "Maybe I don't have enough faith." They are sometimes convinced bad things happen because they did not believe strongly enough.

False Ideas about Faith

Many are convinced that faith is a way of thinking that can somehow manipulate God and change reality. This idea may come from the nineteenth century liberal theology in the United States, which sought to redefine Christianity to make it fit with then-current Freudian ideas about psychology.

Phillips Brooks, pastor of Trinity Episcopal Church in Boston during the late nineteenth century, was one of the first of a line of positive thinkers in America's pulpits. He said, "Believe in yourself and reverence your own human nature; it is the only salvation from brutal vice and every false belief." He said, "The ultimate fact of human life is goodness and not sin." Mary Baker Eddy, founder of Christian Science, took the power of thinking a step further. She denied the existence of matter, evil or sin, disease, and death. Since, according to Eddy, disease does not really exist, the cure for sickness is to come to the realization that the imagined disease is only the result of false belief. She taught that salvation occurred either when a person stopped sinning, or when he stopped believing sin is real.

Some suppose faith is a positive mental attitude, or imagining something to be true until it comes to pass. On this basis, some deny the reality of pain or disease because they think if they deny it to be true, it cannot be true and the "symptoms" will eventually go away.

One theory holds that by "faith," human beings can speak things into existence. Those who hold this view often misinterpret Romans 4:17 to support it, failing to understand that, as the verse says, only God can "call those things which be not as though they were."

To some, faith is visualizing, or mentally picturing, what they would like to happen. They believe if they hold a vivid mental picture long enough, it will come to pass.

Faith Is Not Positive Thinking

There is some value in positive thinking, in having a positive mental attitude, and in thinking about the good things that could be and in visualizing ways to make good things happen, but this is not biblical faith. Biblical faith is trust in God. It is reliance upon Him or confidence in Him. Faith says, "I trust God completely. I believe what He says is absolutely true, and I will continue to trust Him no matter what circumstances say."

The essence of the meaning of the Greek word *pistis*, translated "faith," is *trust*. Hebrews chapter 11 describes faith perfectly as trust in what God has said, and behavior that reflects that trust.

For example, Noah did not say one day, "I think I'll build a boat. I can visualize exactly how I'll build it. After I build this boat, I'll trust God for a flood!" Instead, God commanded Noah to build a boat and he obeyed.

Abraham did not say, "I think I'll sacrifice my son and visualize God raising him from the dead."

Faith is man's response to God's initiative.

The kind of faith described in Hebrews chapter 11 resulted in people being tortured, sawn in half, and imprisoned (Hebrews 11:35-37). This was not the result of mental imaging or positive thinking but of trust in God even in the face of painful and difficult circumstances. For all practical purposes, it would go a long way toward helping us understand the meaning of biblical faith if we would substitute the word "trust" wherever we see the word "faith," for faith is trust in God.

Job said, "Though he slay me, yet will I trust in him" (Job 13:15).

How Faith Is Obtained

Since, according to Romans 3:10-18, human beings are universally incapable of seeking after God by their own initiative, how can faith be obtained? Later in the same letter, Paul wrote, "So then faith cometh by hearing, and hearing by the word of God" (Romans 10:17). By His own sovereign choice, God has arranged it so that when a person hears the Word of God, the ability to believe the Word—to trust that it is true and to rely upon it—accompanies the hearing. It is important to note that this is the *ability* to believe; those who hear the Word can still, if they choose, refuse to believe.

For example, when Paul was on his first missionary journey, accompanied by Barnabas, Jewish leaders in Antioch opposed the message of the gospel. Paul and Barnabas boldly said, "It was necessary that the word of God should first have been spoken to you: but seeing ye put it from you, and judge yourselves unworthy of everlasting life, lo, we turn to the Gentiles (Acts 13:46).

Just as the ability to trust in God and His Word initially comes to a person as he hears the Word of God, so faith increases as he continues to be exposed to the Word of God. In other words, the more of the Word of God we hear, the greater our ability to trust Him. It is important to note, however, that the Greek word *akouo*, a form of which is translated "hearing" in Romans 10:17, has to do with active hearing that results in obedience. In this sense, it is similar to the Hebrew *shema*, translated "hear" in Deuteronomy 6:4. In other words, faith does not come with mere passive hearing; it comes in conjunction with hearing and responding to what one has heard.

How to Live by Faith

Since faith is essentially active trust in God, we live by faith as we demonstrate our trust in Him and His Word by conforming our behavior in obedience to Him. For example, at the beginning of the Christian life, a person demonstrates the genuineness of his faith by repenting of his sins. Since God commands every person everywhere to repent (Acts 17:30), those who genuinely believe in Him and the validity of His Word will repent. Refusal to repent simply demonstrates a lack of genuine faith. Likewise, those who have sincere faith in God will be baptized, for it is a command of Jesus. (See Matthew 28:19; Mark 16:16.) Thus neither repentance nor water baptism are works springing from human initiative by which we seek to earn favor with God; they are the responses of genuine faith by those who trust that the Word of God is true.

So it is throughout the Christian life; as a person grows in grace and in the knowledge of our Lord and Savior Jesus Christ (II Peter 3:18), he will continue—day-by-day—to bring his life into more perfect conformity with the will of God, as expressed in the Word of God. In a very real sense, this is sanctification at work.

The people in the "Hall of Faith" of Hebrews chapter 11 demonstrate the workings of genuine faith, or trust in God.

Faith and Works

Some may think that James disputed Paul's claim that Abraham was justified, not by works, but by faith. (See Romans 4:1-5.) But the problem is merely one of perception. The "faith" of which Paul wrote was a genuine trust in God which resulted in obedience to God's commands; the "faith" of James' letter is at best mental assent with no evidence of genuineness.

In Paul's vocabulary, "works" have to do with activity intended to gain favor with God; James' use of "works" has to do with the natural consequence of genuinely held belief. There is no thought in James' letter that the works resulting from faith somehow enhance one's standing with God. They are simply the logical actions of one who is already in good standing with God.

Paul and James discuss two different events in the life of Abraham. Paul had in mind Abraham's initial response of complete, trusting belief that what God said was true when He said, "Look now toward heaven, and tell the stars, if thou be able to number them . . . So shall thy seed be" (Genesis 15:5). Abraham "believed in the LORD; and he counted it to him for righteousness" (Genesis 15:6). At this point, Abraham did nothing; indeed, there was nothing he could do. God had simply made a promise; Abraham genuinely believed it. Since it was genuine faith, it was accounted to Abraham for righteousness, even though it was impossible at that moment to demonstrate the genuineness of his faith in a tangible way.

But James had in mind the manner in which genuine faith is demonstrated on an on-going basis throughout the life of a believer. He is counteracting those who claim it is possible to possess faith without ever giving evidence of it. No better example could be found than Abraham. Though God did not wait to justify him until he had obediently offered his son, Abraham's obedience to the Lord's command demonstrated the genuineness of the faith he already possessed.

So James is not implying that Abraham was not justified in the sight of God until he offered Isaac on the altar; he is pointing out that Abraham's obedience to God's command demonstrated the validity of his faith and illustrated before men the right standing he already possessed with God.

It is important to note that Abraham did not offer his son in an attempt to earn favor with God. If that had been his motive, James would have condemned his actions, just as would Paul. But for a person who genuinely trusts God, there is no reasonable alternative to obedience to God. Since one has already placed his faith in God, he does not debate on a day-by-day basis whether any specific command of God should be obeyed. If one's trust is in God, there is no other course of action but to obey Him.

Abraham was the friend of God. (See II Chronicles 20:7; Isaiah 41:8.) All who have genuine faith in God have the privilege of being in this relationship with Him. (See John 15:15.)

James 2:24, still addressing the foolish man of James 2:20, points out that it is obvious that right standing with God (justification) does not have to do only with what one believes, but also with what one does as a result of his belief. Indeed, it is what one does that verifies the claim to faith. Even Paul agrees that genuine faith results in works.

Salvation is completely by grace through faith. It does not spring from within us; it is a gift of God and therefore, by definition, completely free. Salvation is not a reward God gives us for religious activity. If it were, we could boast that our accomplishments merited us salvation. Salvation would no longer be a gift, but payment for services rendered. But salvation is not a result of some work we do; it is the work of God. We are, however, created in Christ Jesus for good works. If our salvation is genuine, we will do right things. (See Ephesians 2:8-10.)

It is interesting that James 2:25 offers an example of genuine faith outside of the ancient Hebrew community. James must have had some pertinent reason for offering the two examples he did. How many appropriate examples could have been gleaned from among the Hebrew people in ancient Israel? Why would he choose, as a contrasting example to Abraham, Rahab? There could be no one more unlike Abraham, the chief patriarch, the father of the Hebrew nation. In current vernacular, Rahab had three strikes against her: she was a Gentile, a woman, and a prostitute. But, as startling as it may seem, she had genuine faith in the God of Israel, a faith that demonstrated itself in the risk she took to hide the Israelite spies so as to protect them from the officials of Jericho. (See Joshua 2:1-21; 6:25; Hebrews 11:31.)

The use of these two examples presented the opposite extremities of human experience. If the faith of Abraham and Rahab resulted in specific acts demonstrating their trust in God, so will the faith of everyone else. In a way, to use Abraham and Rahab as examples is like saying that the faith of everyone—from A to Z—will result in works.

Rahab's case was different from that of Abraham in another way. Whereas Abraham received a direct commandment from God to offer his son, Rahab received no such command to hide the spies. She did what she did because it was apparent that it was the right thing to do in the circumstance. This demonstrates that not only will genuine faith express itself in obedience to the overt commands of God, it will also be expressed in the God-honoring decisions common people make on a day-to-day basis.

Biblical faith is not so much a way of thinking as it is genuine trust in God and in the truthfulness of His Word. (See Hebrews 11:6.) This kind of faith results from hearing the Word of God and accepting it as true. And if faith is real, it will without exception result in specific actions demonstrating genuinely held belief, not merely mental assent. Faith is compatible with obedience; it is incompatible with disobedience.

Test Your Knowledge

1. What are the three qualities demonstrating spiritual maturity according to Paul's letters?
2. Name some of the commonly understood, but erroneous definitions of faith.
3. What is one word which best defines faith?
4. Explain the difference between the behavior resulting from genuine faith and works done in an effort to gain favor with God.
5. Discuss the significance of James using Abraham and Rahab as his two examples of true faith.

Apply Your Knowledge

Write a one-page paper explaining the necessity of water baptism as an act of faith rather than as a work meant to earn salvation. Read it before the class next week and use it as a departure for discussion on the difference between things done as a result of faith and things done for the purpose of earning favor with God.

Expand Your Knowledge

Read through the Gospel of John, substituting the word "trust" each time "faith" or "believing" appears. See how this enhances your understanding of biblical faith.

Living with Integrity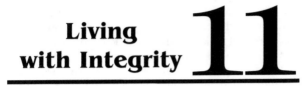

The same came for a witness, to bear witness of the Light, that all men through him might believe.

John 1:7

Start with the Scriptures

Psalm 15   Romans 12:17
Acts 5:1-4; 24:16   II Corinthians 8:21
          Hebrews 13:18

It had been a long, torturous night for Peter. So much of the night had been filled with confusion, turmoil, and fear. It had not started that way. Really, the evening had begun by quietly sharing a meal with Jesus—always a privilege. But everything had gone wrong from the time Jesus had said that one of the twelve would betray Him. Then on the Mount of Olives the Lord had stated that all the disciples would be offended because of Him. It had been more than Peter could understand. Peter remembered what he himself had said. "Though all men shall be offended because of thee, yet will I never be offended" (Matthew 26:33).

Now, as Peter hurried from Pilate's palace, he remembered what Jesus had prophesied concerning his three denials before the cock would crow. He remembered his own boastfulness and how he had fallen asleep in prayer. Nor could he forget the shame he had shown at being associated with Jesus. A strange, passionate fear had seized him. He had even cursed and sworn in an effort to distance himself from the Master.

The Lord uses strange instruments to speak to our consciences. When our mind is thinking otherwise, God stops us short. Just a look of concern from Jesus, just a rooster's crowing, and suddenly Peter saw what he had done. More important than that, the disciple saw what he actually was.

Deep, convulsive sobbing broke the morning stillness. The heart of the fisherman had been broken. The brashness was gone now. The self-assurance had crumbled. In their place was only an agony of mind and spirit.

Was it just Peter who needed this honest appraisal? Or do we, who are so quick to judge others, also need God to judge our hearts? Our own standards of measurement are often inaccurate. We need God's Word and His Spirit to judge properly. David cried out to the Lord, "Search me, O God, and know my heart: try me, and know my thoughts: And see if there be any wicked way in me, and lead me in the way everlasting" (Psalm 139:23-24).

Let God Be True

While working as a clerk in a store in New Salem, Illinois, Abraham Lincoln discovered that a woman one day had paid a few cents more than what she owed on her bill. That very night he walked six miles to return the difference. Later, after buying into the store business with a partner, Lincoln ran into serious financial problems. The business failed. His partner died. But Lincoln paid off his own heavy burden of debt and that of his partner's. No doubt this experience helped to establish his reputation as "Honest Abe."

As a boy Abraham Lincoln spent less than a year in schools in Kentucky and Indiana, but he taught himself to read. Over and over he read from his small stock of books, which included the Bible. By the hearth fire, young Lincoln must have learned of the God who is always true.

This one attribute of God—His honesty—should be an inspiration to us all. For the Lord to be trustworthy, He must be true. There can be no change in this divine characteristic. He is "the Father of lights, with whom is no variableness, neither shadow of turning" (James 1:17). God must always be true to His Word and always faithful to His promises. All His assertions must be correct. God cannot lie. (See Titus 1:2.)

In the day that we live, perhaps it is difficult for some to believe that there is an all-seeing, virtuous God. Science and technology appear to be the gods of modern education. If we go to the popular book stores, we may have a problem finding a Bible. However, we certainly will have no difficulty finding publications on the occult or the New Age movement. If we go to many mainline churches, we will see little more than empty rituals. If we go to hospitals and medical clinics, we will discover that thousands of unborn babies are being aborted.

Despite the lack of morals in our day, God does not change. As the apostle Paul explained to some of the early Christians, a lack of faith on the part of the Jews or anyone else does not alter the Lord. "What if some did not believe and were without faith? Does their lack of faith and their faithlessness nullify and make ineffective and void the faithfulness of God and His fidelity [to His Word]? By no means! Let God be found true though every human being be false and a liar, as it is written, That You may be justified and shown to be upright in what You say, and prevail when You are judged [by sinful men]" (Romans 3:3-4, *The Amplified Bible*).

Everywhere one looks in the Bible he will see the integrity of God, but it is probably no more evident than when seen in contrast with the dishonesty of men. There were individuals like Jacob who took advantage of others but to whom the Lord granted unalterable promises. Rachel stole her father's images, Simeon and Levi tricked the Shechemites, and David had Uriah murdered to cover his own sin. While the Word of God tells of these deceptions, we know that they were far from what the Lord wanted. With the death of Uriah, for instance, it looked as if David had fooled almost everyone. "But the thing that David had done displeased the LORD" (II Samuel 11:27).

One of those who stand out as being deceitful, in sharp contrast to God Himself, was Balaam, the prophet from Mesopotamia. At first Balaam refused to follow the messengers of King Balak back to Moab for the purpose of cursing Israel. But despite the Lord's clear warning to Balaam, that prophet began to reconsider his initial decision. II Peter 2:15 says he "loved the wages of unrighteousness." Neither the voice of a donkey nor the voice of an angel could set Balaam straight, but God was faithful to Israel, and He would not allow Balaam to pronounce anything except blessing upon His people.

Instead of cursing Israel, as Balak had demanded, the wayward prophet declared that the Lord's hand of protection would remain in place. Balaam saw a glorious future. God prophesied through Balaam that Israel would endure as a unique people, a fact that has proven itself over the centuries. "For from the top of the rocks I see him, and from the hills I behold him: lo, the people shall dwell alone, and shall not be reckoned among the nations" (Numbers 23:9).

If King Balak had hopes that God might somehow change His mind, then they were soon destroyed by another statement from Balaam. "God is not a man, that he should lie; neither the son of man, that he should repent: hath he said, and shall he not do it? or hath he spoken, and shall he not make it good?" (Numbers 23:19).   Obviously Balaam could be bribed and persuaded to do evil, but absolutely nothing could influence God to do the same.

Knowing that God is completely honest sets the highest of moral standards for all those who wish to walk in His ways. Honesty is required to approach Him and to please Him. We can have no close relationship with the Lord while we walk in darkness. "But if we walk in the light, as he is in the light, we have fellowship one with another, and the blood of Jesus Christ his Son cleanseth us from all sin" (I John 1:7).

Heaven is a prepared place for a prepared people. "And there shall in no wise enter into it any thing that . . . maketh a lie" (Revelation 21:27). The holy city is reserved exclusively for honest people. The Holy Spirit reemphasized the fact: "For without are dogs, and sorcerers, and whoremongers, and murderers, and idolaters, and whosoever loveth and maketh a lie" (Revelation 22:15).

Honest with Yourself

Anyone who wishes to be right with God will have to come face to face with a shocking reality. He must see himself for what he really is. Every pretense will have to be laid aside. All disguises will have to be discarded. There can be no misrepresentations, no distortions. A person must first be honest with himself. There is just no way for an individual to find God without an honest heart.

Why do people struggle so desperately to avoid being self-exposed? Jesus said that "men loved darkness rather than light, because their deeds were evil. For every one that doeth evil hateth the light, neither cometh to the light, lest his deeds should be reproved" (John 3:19-20). Just as thieves prefer the darkness to commit their crimes, so guilty sinners avoid the gospel light.

The strongest denunciation that Jesus uttered during His earthly ministry was aimed at religious pretense. The word "hypocrite," with which He described the scribes and Pharisees, must have cut them deeply. The word not only suggested that these religionists were "play-acting" but strongly stated that they were "godless." They were, like the many tombs that were white-washed in Jerusalem just before the Passover, beautiful on the outside but full of dead men's bones. Men still masquerade and wear masks. They still deceive others. There are still those who profess to know God but deny Him by the way they live. There remain those who are more concerned with outward performance than inward holiness.

What a challenge we face in these days to be genuine! It is so easy to judge another for doing something wrong when we ourselves are doing far worse, counting the splinters in the eye of someone else while we have a log-jam in our own. Jesus said, "Thou hypocrite, first cast out the beam out of thine own eye; and then shalt thou see clearly to cast out the mote out of thy brother's eye" (Matthew 7:5).

The Deceptive Web

Telling the truth can be painful for the moment, but the long-term rewards are tremendous. There will be no need to shred the evidence when we speak the truth; nor will we need to perjure ourselves in the court of our own conscience. There will be a freedom to look everyone in the eye, a sense that we have done the decent thing, a knowledge that we have maintained our highest principles.

Liars are guilty of fraud. A falsehood is told to gain an unfair advantage of others or to escape the consequence of a misdeed. There are no "little, white lies." Someone—our landlord, our doctor, our spouse, our pastor—is being injured by our dishonesty and disrespect. We may imagine all manner of reasons for telling an untruth, but in the end, we are breaking the Golden Rule and violating the Scriptures. No one wants to be lied to.

Nor are all lies spoken by the lips. We can simply gloss over the truth and keep silent when we know we should speak out. We can give the wrong impression without speaking a word. Courts of law demand that witnesses speak "the whole truth and nothing but the truth."

Perhaps the person who suffers the most from deception is the individual who tries "to pull it off." He is the one most grossly deceived. He has allowed the enemy of his soul to lead him astray. The devil himself "abode not in the truth, because there is no truth in him" (John 8:44). Satan will weave his deceptive web over anyone who will walk in his ways.

What a personal cost to an individual if he lives a lie! He is sure to become entangled in one untruth after another until there seems no way out.

David, though a man after God's own heart, got caught in the web of deceit. It started with a lustful look at his neighbor's wife and continued on after the act of adultery. It spread further and further, affecting even the innocent. David called Uriah from the battlefield in an attempt to cover his own sin and shame. When this failed, he plotted to have the gallant soldier murdered. Uriah was entrusted with his own death warrant, and the matter seemed to have been laid to rest by David's conscience. But problems for David had only begun, as they do for all those who take this ignoble course.

Sometimes we may feel, because our doctrine is right, our life is also right. Obviously we should believe the truth, but integrity goes far deeper than that. We must be honest in our everyday activities, in our business dealings, and even in our thoughts. We must avoid those things that even look dishonorable. "Providing for honest things, not only in the sight of the Lord, but also in the sight of men" (II Corinthians 8:21).

The words "Urim" and "Thummim" hold a fascination for many Bible scholars, for while it is certain they were two parts in the ceremonial breastplate worn by the high priest, we do not know exactly how these objects were used. Major decisions were sometimes delayed "till there stood up a priest with Urim and Thummim" (Nehemiah 7:65). How interesting to note, as T. W. Engstrom has pointed out, that the Hebrew word *thom*, the singular form of *thummim*, is translated as "integrity" in such verses of Scripture as Genesis 20:5-6; I Kings 9:4; Job 2:3, 9! *Strong's Exhaustive Concordance* indicates that *thummim* means "complete truth." Even as the high priest was required to wear the special breastplate over his heart, we who are the Lord's foot soldiers are to put on "the breastplate of righteousness" (Ephesians 6:14).

It is easy to be influenced by the unethical standards of the world. It is so easy to adopt an "everybody-does-it" attitude that even Christians can be ensnared in the devil's web. At a time when everything from traffic laws to marriage vows are broken with impunity, the pressure is on. And once we begin to compromise our convictions with what someone called "the small departures from truth," it becomes easier to forget our accountability to God. The little foxes "spoil the vines" (Song of Solomon 2:15).

A young boy came home with an item he had "lifted" in a local store. The parents attended a Pentecostal church, but they laughed at their son's small impropriety. When the lad became a man, however, he became a habitual thief.

It Could Have Been Different

It could have been different for Achan. He was of the tribe of Judah, the foremost of all the tribes both in march and in battle. One day Christ would come as "the Lion of the tribe of Juda" (Revelation 5:5). It was no small thing for Achan to have followed a leader like Joshua and to have seen firsthand the victory that God had given to Israel at Jericho.

It could have been different, but Achan "took of the accursed thing: and the anger of the LORD was kindled against the children of Israel" (Joshua 7:1). What a price the nation paid because one man coveted and hid an attractive Babylonish garment, two hundred shekels of silver, and a wedge of gold! Our weakest moment often comes just after a tremendous victory. Our mighty Jericho has fallen, but our little Ai routs us. We have allowed some secret dishonesty to go unchecked and unconquered in our lives.

How extremely different it might have been for Ananias and Sapphira if they had only been honest. Outwardly this man and his wife appeared dedicated and liberal. Inwardly they were deceptive and grasping. Their sin lay in pretending that they had given all the money from the sale of their property. What a lesson we can learn from the statement that they "kept back part of the price" (Acts 5:2)! No, God does not strike down every hypocrite in the church, but His judgment upon Ananias and Sapphira serves as ample warning to all who try to deceive others.

Some would say that Judas could not have done differently, that he was a victim of fate. But God holds every man responsible for his own actions. This disciple's crime appears all the more heinous when we realize that he had the privilege of walking in close fellowship with Jesus Christ for three years. Sorrowfully the Lord asked him, "Judas, betrayest thou the Son of man with a kiss?" (Luke 22:48). That kiss had been devised by Judas as a cunning sign to Christ's enemies, but by this one despicable gesture, the disciple brought reproach on his name forever. Hester H. Cholmondoly wrote, "For thirty pieces of silver, Judas sold himself, not Christ."

Sincerity on Trial

We usually identify sincere people as those who are genuine and true. They can be counted on. They will do all they have said, and perhaps even more. Their handshake is their pledge; their word is as good as gold.

The word "sincere" is derived from the Latin *sin*, meaning "without," and *caries*, indicating "decay." It means to be free from adulteration, to be pure and honest. This is a quality possessed by God Himself. (W. E. Vine points out that II Corinthians 1:12 can be translated the "sincerity of God.") Certainly it is a characteristic that the Lord expects in His people.

A missionary on deputation in North America asked a pastor if he knew a good mechanic. The missionary had been told in another town that the ball joints and tie-rod ends in his van needed repair, which would cost over two hundred dollars. The pastor took the missionary to a mechanic who ran his own shop. After careful inspection it was obvious that, while some wear was evident, the repairs were not needed. The mechanic's bill was five dollars.

Everywhere it seems that sincerity is on trial. Politicians and ministers are distrusted because of past scandals. Money is passed under the table. Odometer readings are set back. Immigration papers are falsified. Income tax reports are doctored. Expense accounts are padded.

Someone has observed that integrity is tested during prosperity. For many the test has proven too difficult. They found it easier to be honest when they had fewer business investments and personal possessions. A wise man wrote these words, "Remove far from me vanity and lies: give me neither poverty nor riches; feed me with food convenient for me: lest I be full, and deny thee, and say, Who is the LORD? or lest I be poor, and steal, and take the name of my God in vain" (Proverbs 30:8-9).

In the sacred halls of our own conscience, we are being tested. There are countless opportunities to prove our sincerity or, on the other hand, to prove our dishonesty. At times someone—a pastor or a Christian friend—may be there to help us make the proper decision. At other times no one may be present to take the witness stand except God and ourselves.

Joseph was certainly more concerned with the Lord's approval than any other. During what may have been his greatest temptation, a temptation to commit adultery, he asked, "How then can I do this great wickedness, and sin against God?" (Genesis 39:9). A person must be true to his conscience and to the Word of God. There are no higher courts of appeal.

Test Your Knowledge

True or False:

1. Peter had cursed and sworn in an effort to distance himself from Jesus. _____

2. We all need to do an honest appraisal of ourselves. _____

3. Abraham Lincoln felt he should be an honest shopkeeper. _____

4. God turned a blind eye to those who were dishonest in the Bible. _____

5. Balaam cursed Israel. _____

6. Knowing that God is completely honest sets the highest of moral standards for those who walk in His ways. _____

7. There is no way for an individual to find God without an honest heart. _____

8. There is no pain associated with telling the truth. _____

9. Not all lies are spoken by the lips. _____

10. God will kill every hypocrite in the church. _____

Apply Your Knowledge

There is hope when you fail to be completely honest. What steps may you take toward sincerity? Take time to evaluate such passages of Scripture as I John 1:8-2:2; Psalm 103:3; Matthew 6:14. Remember that the Comforter is given to lead you into all truth. He is the Spirit of truth and will help you understand God's ways.

We should also be reminded that it is Satan's objective to bring the innocent under condemnation. He is the accuser of the brethren.

Expand Your Knowledge

All integrity is based on the principle of accountability. Before reading the next chapter consider your responsibility to God and to men.

More Than Money

Let a man so account of us, as of the ministers of Christ, and stewards of the mysteries of God. Moreover it is required in stewards, that a man be found faithful.

I Corinthians 4:1-2

Living in the Spirit affects every aspect of our lives, including the routine of our daily activities and the use of all resources that are entrusted to us. True spirituality involves not only the mystical and the unseen, but it is clearly reflected in our behavior toward God, family, others, and ourselves. To paraphrase James, the apostle of practicality, the only way you will see my faith is through the things that I do. (See James 2:18.)

It is common in our world for individuals to experience feelings of frustration and emptiness in life.

They often complain that there seems to be no purpose or real substance in spite of much busyness. It is almost as if they were running hard on a giant treadmill that takes them nowhere. This is because they have ignored the Giver of life and His blueprint for a successful life. True fulfillment is found in living for God.

A life devoted to God must go far beyond mere lip service. It must recognize the heavenly Father as the giver of all good gifts and use those gifts in His service and for His glory. Our time, abilities, possessions, and finances need to be submitted to the lordship of Jesus Christ. Then we can know the sheer joy of a life lived in harmony with His divine plan.

What Is Stewardship?

The basic definition of a *steward* is "a person who manages another's property or financial affairs, or who administers anything as the agent of another." We commonly associate the term with the proper use of money, but it actually involves much more. In his book *The Life I Owe*, William J. Keech says, "Christian stewardship is the dedication of all I am and have, under the control of God's Spirit, to the doing of His will, in recognition of His lordship, in gratitude for His love, in every area of my life, and in the service of His redemptive fellowship."

The first principle that we must confront and accept is that we are stewards and not owners. It is true that during a lifetime of diligent effort many possessions, talents, abilities, and finances will pass through our hands. But, as Paul preached in Athens, we must remember that it is "God that made the world and all things therein" (Acts 17:24). This is echoed in Psalm 24:1, "The earth is the LORD's, and the fulness thereof; the world, and they that dwell therein."

A story is told of a minister who was driving down a country lane when he noticed a farmer working in a large garden. The minister pulled over and got out of his vehicle to talk with the farmer. Admiring the straight, healthy green rows, the crops free of insects and weeds, and the luscious produce on the vines, the minister remarked, "My friend, the Lord has really blessed you with a beautiful garden." The farmer straightened up from his hoeing, looked around and said, "Yeah, He has; but you should've seen it when He had it by Himself."

This humorous story illustrates several points. The minister was correct in observing that the garden, and even the fruit of the garden, belonged to the Lord. But the farmer was stating that, as a good steward, he had taken what the Lord provided and worked to make it the best he could. He had planted the seed, applied the pesticide, and carefully removed the weeds. But it was God who created the soil and the nutrients in it, put life in the seed, allowed the sun to shine, and sent the rain in its proper season. And so we should take the life that God has given us, and the blessings He sends, and work to make it the best for His glory.

In *What the Bible Says about Stewardship*, A. Q. Van Benshoten, Jr., lists four affirmations concerning stewardship that are worthy of consideration:

Stewardship Affirmation 1. God is the Creator and Owner. God is Giver, Redeemer, and Sustainer of all. (See Genesis 1:1-2:4; 12:1-3; Psalm 24; Colossians 1:15-23; Hebrews 1:1-3.)

Stewardship Affirmation 2. Each person is a steward; all he or she possesses is a trust from the Creator. (See I Chronicles 29:1-18; Isaiah 42:5-7; 49:6; Luke 2:28-34; I Corinthians 4:1-5; II Corinthians 8:1-9; I Peter 4:10-11.)

Stewardship Affirmation 3. Each person must acknowledge his or her stewardship before God in this life. (See Luke 12:48; 24:45-49; Acts 1:6-11; I Corinthians 4:2; 6:19-20.)

Stewardship Affirmation 4. Each person must ultimately give an account to God of his or her stewardship. (See Genesis 3:9-11; Isaiah 45:23-46:5; Luke 16:1-13; Romans 14:10-12.)

The position of a steward is one of responsibility and honor. David expressed his awe at the confidence God has placed in us in one of his beautiful songs: "When I consider thy heavens, the work of thy fingers, the moon and the stars, which thou hast ordained; What is man, that thou art mindful of him? . . . Thou madest him to have dominion over the works of thy hands; thou hast put all things under his feet" (Psalm 8:3-6).

Part of spiritual growth and maturity is realizing our obligation to God as stewards. We have received and will receive many blessings from the Lord. These are not to be squandered, nor are they merely for personal enjoyment. These gifts have been entrusted to us by our Father, and we have a responsibility to invest and use them in a manner that will bring Him glory and advance the cause of His kingdom.

Time—An Indication of Priorities

The *Random House College Dictionary* lists sixty-one major definitions of the word "time." It may be somewhat difficult to express the meaning of time, but we all understand this precious commodity that has been given to each person. "If only there were more time" and "I just don't have the time" are common expressions. But the truth is we are all given twenty-four hours a day and seven days a week. The way in which we use this time is a reflection of our discipline and our priorities.

Realizing that our time is actually a gift entrusted to us by God, we must exercise wise stewardship of this limited resource. We can take scriptural principles regarding proper priorities and determine the most prudent and beneficial use of our time. Certainly God should occupy the number one spot on our list: "But seek ye first the kingdom of God, and his righteousness; and all these things shall be added unto you" (Matthew 6:33).

Our communion with God through prayer is the lifeline of the Christian walk and must take precedence over less meaningful uses of our time. The Scriptures are filled with exhortations to prayer: "That men ought always to pray, and not to faint" (Luke 18:1); "Praying always . . ." (Ephesians 6:18); "Continue in prayer" (Colossians 4:2); and "Pray without ceasing" (I Thessalonians 5:17). These are but a few of the passages in the Bible that stress the significance of a consistent prayer life.

Another vital aspect of our time spent with the Lord concerns the reading, meditation, and application of the Word of God. Psalm 119 is filled with beautiful statements of the power and importance of the Scriptures. "Wherewithal shall a young man cleanse his way? by taking heed thereto according to thy word" (Psalm 119:9). "Thy word have I hid in mine heart, that I might not sin against thee" (Psalm 119:11). Paul exhorted his son in the gospel, "Till I come, give attendance to reading, to exhortation, to doctrine" (I Timothy 4:13).

Spiritual growth and maturity cannot be attained apart from the study of the Bible. Mere passage of time will not cause a person to grow in Christ. Growth occurs only as we feed on the unfailing wisdom of the Word and progress from milk to meat in scriptural truths.

Another high priority on the list of wise use of time is our family. The family was the first institution established by God and is the basic building block of society. Healthy family relationships between spouses and between parents and children require a hearty dose of time. Too often, careers and other objectives are pursued at the expense of family. To achieve the world's definition of success at the expense of our family, however, is really not accomplishment at all.

Children grow up quickly and the opportunities to share the joy of discovery and growth can never be reclaimed. The issues of the moment can often be placed on hold so that we can take time to see the world through our child's eyes and share their wonder. These are priceless moments, essential to forming a lasting bond of closeness with this valuable heritage from God, our children.

Frequently, however, husbands and wives focus all family time on the children and neglect to spend time building their own relationship. One day the children are grown, the nest is empty, and another thirty, forty or more years together lie before them. This can be either an extremely rewarding season of life or a very challenging time.

One of the reasons this is a difficult period for some is that they have never invested much time in building the bond of closeness with their spouse. But if through the years of struggle, raising a family, building a career, and getting established in life, they have made each other a priority, they will be far more excited about the later years.

On the list of important uses of our time we must certainly include selfless service to others. Striving to reach the unsaved, reaching out to the less fortunate, and helping the unsuspecting provide some of life's richest rewards. Jesus Christ, our ultimate example, devoted His earthly ministry to helping others. We need to share His vision and heartbeat. In the story of the Good Samaritan, the priest and the Levite did not have time for the wounded man. But the true neighbor, the Samaritan, went out of his way to meet the needs of the one who was hurt. Jesus said this demonstrates the love we should have for others.

We must also take time for ourselves. Taken in its proper context, this is very important time. Time spent in study and self-improvement will pay dividends many times over. This is like a gardener sharpening his hoe; it is not wasted time, for it can serve to make us more effective in many areas of life. We may be falling short of our potential in life because we have become content in our comfort zone and are not putting forth the effort to fully develop the talents that God has given us.

And there must be time for rest. Jesus told the disciples, "Come ye yourselves apart into a desert place, and rest a while" (Mark 6:31). To use most effectively the energy and strength with which the Lord has blessed us, we must have proper rest. Vance Havner once observed that we should "come apart lest we come apart."

The same amount of time is given to each individual in any given day. We should work to use this time in the wisest manner possible, realizing that we have no guarantee of the number of days that will be allotted to each of us. But "when time shall be no more," and we stand before our Lord, we want to know that we have been faithful in our stewardship of time.

You Are Gifted

Every person is gifted and every person has areas of weakness. A cartoon illustrating this showed a building with a sign that proclaimed, "Midvale School for the Gifted." A student was trying to enter the building and was pushing fervently on a door that was labeled, "Please pull." This may cause us to chuckle, but it accurately demonstrates that exceptional ability in one area may be accompanied by weaknesses in other areas. It is important to realize that each of us is a special creation of the Master and has been blessed with unique and valuable talents.

Our area of giftedness may be intelligence, personality, perseverance, compassion, loyalty, or some other equally important virtue. We need not underestimate the incomparable worth of our special talents and abilities. These are gifts from God and, as stewards, we have a responsibility to develop and use them for His glory.

When we speak of gifts that God has given to Christians, we usually think of the spiritual gifts listed in I Corinthians 12:8-10. These are indeed gifts that God has blessed the church with, but these are not the only gifts the Scriptures mention. We find ministry gifts in Ephesians 4:11, which we refer to as the five-fold ministry. And in Romans 12:6-8 and I Corinthians 12:28 we find reference to other gifts that have been called the service gifts. The author of *So You Want to Serve* lists nine service gifts: prophecy, giving, encouragement, leadership, mercy, serving, teaching, administration, and helping.

Not everyone fits into the realm of ministry described in Ephesians 4:11. But every child of God is called and equipped for areas of service in the kingdom of God. It is our responsibility to recognize this giftedness and work to refine and improve our effectiveness in this ministry or ministries. It would be a grave mistake for us to compare ourselves to someone else. Very likely, they are blessed with different talents and gifts. Proper stewardship requires each individual to measure his own life against the potential of what he can be in Christ and reach for that full potential.

We Can't Forget Money

The Word of the Lord has a great deal to say about the subject of money. I Timothy 6:10 warns us that "the love of money is the root of all evil." Money itself is not an evil medium; it can be used for worthwhile causes. But the wrong attitude toward money can cause a person to err from the truth. Therefore it is imperative that we study and heed what the Scriptures have to say concerning this important subject.

From the very first book of the Bible God established a principle to remind us of divine ownership—the principle of tithing. Actually, everything we have belongs to God, and to reinforce this in our consciousness we are to give the first tenth of all our increase to the Lord. Above and beyond this, God allows for freewill offerings as an expression of love and sacrifice.

Tithing is a direct and definite command of the Word, and it is our obligation to obey without complaining or doubting. But the beauty of our Lord is that He has promised bountiful blessings for those who follow His plan in faith. "Honour the LORD with thy substance, and with the firstfruits of all thine increase: So shall thy barns be filled with plenty, and thy presses shall burst out with new wine" (Proverbs 3:9-10). "Bring ye all the tithes into the storehouse, that there may be meat in mine house, and prove me now herewith, saith the LORD of hosts, if I will not open you the windows of heaven, and pour you out a blessing, that there shall not be room enough to receive it" (Malachi 3:10).

Time and again we have seen the testimony of God's blessing in the lives of those who have been faithful to the plan of God on a consistent basis. As they continue to honor God and bless the work of God, He continues to pour out blessings upon them.

In his book *Financing the Lord's Church*, A. J. Wall listed five scriptural guidelines for giving that are worthy of our consideration.

1. One's giving should be through the church (Malachi 3:10).

2. One's giving should be cheerful (II Corinthians 9:7).

3. One's giving should be sacrificial (II Corinthians 8:2).

4. One's giving should be systematic (I Corinthians 16:2).

5. One's giving should be to honor God (Proverbs 3:9).

Not only does the Bible give us guidelines concerning giving, it also touches on our relationship to money in other ways. We are exhorted in Romans 12:11 to be "not slothful in business." An important part of our testimony is that we handle our finances and obligations in a responsible and forthright manner. Certainly the child of God should have a reputation for paying his bills and avoiding wasteful spending and unnecessary debt. Not only will these things become heavy weights, but they will hinder an effective testimony.

A good steward is obligated to employ wise management practices, and this includes the finances that God has entrusted us with. We are not all expected to be Wall Street wizards, but we can master the art of consistent savings and preparing for unforeseen emergencies and the possibility of retirement. A properly constructed budget, placing God first and covering these other contingencies, will be an invaluable tool in mastering proper stewardship of our money.

Stewards Must Give an Account

A basic tenet of stewardship is accountability. Paul wrote in I Corinthians 4:2, "It is required in stewards, that a man be found faithful." A point of evaluation will come for each of us concerning our role as stewards. Romans 14:12 tells us, "So then every one of us shall give account of himself to

God." In light of this certainty, we must commit ourselves to continual improvement in the areas of stewardship.

Jesus gave us what is often called the parable of the talents in Matthew 25:14-30. The third servant in this parable took the talent that was given him and buried it in the earth. Because he made no effort to develop that which was left in his trust, he was called a wicked and slothful servant and received harsh judgment. This comes as a clear warning to us not to take the matter of stewardship lightly or ignore the responsibility we have been given.

A beautiful description of faithful stewardship and its reward is seen in Paul's last letter to Timothy. The great apostle had received the glorious gospel, had devoted all his God-given talents and abilities to the furtherance of it, and had touched the lives of countless multitudes. As he neared the end of his life's journey, Paul reflected on his role as a steward: "I have fought a good fight, I have finished my course, I have kept the faith: henceforth there is laid up for me a crown of righteousness, which the Lord, the righteous judge, shall give me at that day: and not to me only, but unto all them also that love his appearing" (II Timothy 4:7-8).

All stewards must one day give an account. To the slothful, judgment is promised. But to the faithful stewards, who in godly fear sought to use God's gifts for His glory, a tremendous reward awaits.

Christian stewardship is the dedication of all we have and are to the performing of the will of the Master. When followed from a heart of faith, this is a lifestyle that will provide for a purposeful, fulfilled life. It lifts the focus from self and places it upon God, where it belongs.

Knowing that all stewards will be called upon to give an account, let us commit ourselves to the highest standards of service in the kingdom of God. God is always faithful, and rich rewards are in store for those who make the commitment to let Jesus Christ be Lord of every facet of life.

Test Your Knowledge

1. Based on the material in the lesson, how would you define stewardship?

2. What are some areas of our lives where good stewardship is required?

3. List different types of service gifts from Romans 12:6-8 and I Corinthians 12:28.

4. Give scriptural references that promise God's blessings upon those who honor Him with their finances.

5. "It is required in stewards, that a man be found _____" (I Corinthians 4:2).

Apply Your Knowledge

How well have you been fulfilling the duties of a steward with the time, abilities, and resources that have been given you? If you find that you have not done as well as you should, do not dwell on mistakes of the past. Instead, determine to apply yourself to the consistent development of scriptural practices. The Christian walk is one in which we are always striving to grow more into the likeness of Christ.

Expand Your Knowledge

The Bible has much to say about our responsibilities as stewards. Study the teachings of the Word on this vital subject and understand how they apply not only in finances but in every area of our lives. After you have established a biblical foundation, there are a number of good books that deal with stewardship from the Christian perspective.

Patience and Contentment 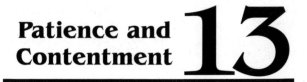13

In your patience possess ye your souls.
Luke 21:19

One of the most valuable Christian virtues is patience. It is, however, often one of the most difficult to practice. Ordinarily, it seems much easier to be *doing* something than merely *waiting*. But the writer of Hebrews put it this way: "For ye have need of patience, that, after ye have done the will of God, ye might receive the promise" (Hebrews 10:36). In other words, after we have done everything it is God's will for us to do, all that remains is to wait on His timing.

After explaining the painful experiences believers will have just before the Second Coming, Jesus said, "In your patience possess ye your souls" (Luke 21:19). The only thing believers can do in the face of persecution, betrayal, and hatred (Luke 21:12-17) is to wait patiently for deliverance from God. To seek revenge is not an option. (See Romans 12:14, 17-21.)

Some of the greatest heroes of faith in Scripture demonstrated patience in the face of intense pressure.

The Patience of Job

An entire book of the Old Testament is given to preserving the story of the life of Job, an ancient believer who was a contemporary of Abraham. Job, who lived in the days before any written revelation was given, had very limited revelation compared with the Israelites and certainly with the New Testament church. Yet he is held up as an example of patience even to Spirit-filled believers. (See James 5:11.)

The Book of Job describes, but does not explain, the undeserved suffering of a righteous man (Job 1:1, 8; 2:3). Though a large part of the book is given to expressions of the theory of retribution (Job 3:1-37:24), God never revealed to Job the cause of his suffering. Instead, He asked, "Who is he that hideth counsel without knowledge?" (Job 42:3).

The reader is given the insight into the mysterious events in the throne room of heaven; Satan came into the presence of God and was drawn by the Lord into a conversation that had devastating consequences for innocent Job (Job 1:6-12; 2:1-6). Job did not have access to this information, but doubtless it would not have been helpful to him if he had; the fact that the Lord suggested Job to Satan complicates any idea that a law of retribution is at work.

Job's friends were convinced that there was a direct connection between his suffering and some great sin he had committed, which he had yet to confess. Job agreed that there should be a direct link between sin and suffering, but he complained that in his case his theory failed (chapters 21, 23-24). He had done everything right (Job 1:1, 5, 8, 22; 2:3, 10), but he suffered the loss he thought was reserved for the wicked.

It seems significant that Satan has a high profile in the instigation of Job's sufferings but that he is absent from the events surrounding the end of the suffering and the reinstitution of blessing. If the law of retribution had been at work, it seems that God would have permitted Satan to try him in response to some specific sin and when Job had been sufficiently chastised, Satan would have been recalled. But God offered no reason for singling Job out, other than that he was a perfect man, and He offered no rationale for the conclusion of the suffering.

The wisdom arising from Job is that God is sovereign and that He has no obligation to explain Himself or His actions to men. Even in the midst of unexplained and undeserved suffering, men are to honor God. Indeed, men find freedom only as they acknowledge God's freedom and as they refrain from demanding that God operate according to human rules. The Book of Job utterly refutes the notion of a mechanistic, impersonal universe. A simple truth is revealed in the most dramatic terms: men need God more than answers.

In the only reference to Job in the New Testament, James offered him as an example of the patience that believers should possess. The translation of James 5:11 offered by the NKJV is helpful: "Indeed we count them blessed who endure. You have heard of the perseverance of Job and seen the end intended by the Lord—that the Lord is very compassionate and merciful."

Endurance of suffering has its own reward. As pointed out in James 1:2-4, endurance of trials produces patience. Paul agreed. (See Romans 5:3.) Since patience is a much-needed virtue, the person who faces and endures trials is blessed; his trial is an opportunity to mature in a vital area of character development. As Paul pointed out in his description of the fruit of the Spirit, long-suffering is evidence of the indwelling Spirit. (See Galatians 5:22-23.)

James' readers knew well the story of Job. This gives valuable insight as to the intent and purpose of the Book of Job: to demonstrate that the Lord is compassionate and merciful, and that He intends good for His children. Job lived prior to the giving of the law of Moses, and the book reveals that the law of retribution is not at work; people do not always get what they deserve. This was certainly the case with the oppressed poor that James addressed. But the Book of Job also reveals that even though a godly person may endure unjust suffering, God is aware of it and intends ultimate good to come out of it. In Job's case, his family was restored to him, and his material wealth was twice what it was before his suffering began. (See Job 42:10-17.)

This should be an encouragement to James' readers. If God deals with them as He did with Job, they will in the end receive far richer rewards than the mere wages of which they haved been defrauded.

Trials Produce Patience

Patience is the first and one of the foremost virtues commended by James. (See James 1:2-4.) But the trial of one's faith produces patience only when the trial is accepted and endured by faith. The essence of faith is trust in God. Again, Job is the example. In the midst of his trial of faith, Job confessed, "Though he slay me, yet will I trust in him" (Job 13:15).

In its purest form, patience is possible only when one accepts the difficult circumstance to be allowed by God and useful to God in the shaping of one's character. Character is more important than comfort.

In James 1:4, the Greek *teleios*, translated "perfect," implies "maturity" when applied to human beings, not moral perfection. No human being will reach the point in this life where there is no further room for improvement. The goal of conformity to the image of the Son of God (Romans 8:29) is high enough to always hold a still greater challenge for even the most mature. Even Paul, toward the end of his life, did not count himself to have attained his full potential in Christ. (See Philippians 3:12.)

A necessary prerequisite to maturity is the development of patience; no one is mature without it. Impatience, with its attendant impulsiveness and testiness, is an indication of immaturity. James encouraged his readers to "let patience have her perfect work." That is, they were to allow patience to run its full course.

Bill Gothard defined patience as "accepting a difficult situation from God without giving Him a deadline to remove it." Patience can be developed only in response to painful, unpleasant experiences. The person who has learned to trust God though he can see no reason for or solution to his problems is a "perfect and entire" person who "wants nothing." This terminology exalts patience to one of the chief virtues.

In Romans 5:3, Paul wrote, "We glory in tribulations also: knowing that tribulation worketh patience." Not only does the assurance of justification and consequent peace with God enable us to stand and to rejoice in hope (Romans 5:1-2), it also enables us to glory in tribulations. The word *tribulation* means "pressure." Why does the knowledge of our justification enable us to glory in the pressures of life? Those who are not aware of their right standing with God often think life's pressures are somehow evidence that God is not happy with them. They interpret problems and difficulties as signs that God has forsaken them or that He is punishing them. But when a person is assured of his right standing with God, he knows that problems and pressures are no sign of God's displeasure with him, and he is able to respond to the difficulties of life in a more productive way.

Since the pressures of life, responded to in the right way, tend to produce certain desirable character qualities, those who are certain of their right standing with God can "glory" or rejoice in these problems. One result of right response to the pressures of life is patience. Those who have never been able to accept life's problems and to work through them are generally shallow, short-tempered, irritable individuals who lose control of their emotions when things do not go their way. But those who have learned that even though life is not fair, God is still faithful, can accept the difficulties of life with grace and look for the potential good through the pain.

In Romans 15:4, Paul wrote, "For whatsoever things were written aforetime were written for our learning, that we through patience and comfort of the scriptures might have hope." Paul's statement here seems to anticipate a question from his Jewish audience. If it is true that ethnic Jewishness offers no salvific advantage (Romans 2:26-29), and if the law of Moses terminated with the coming of the Messiah (Romans 10:4), of what use are the Hebrew Scriptures? Should they be disregarded?

Paul's answer, in part, is that "whatsoever things

were written aforetime were written for our learning." This is similar to his statement elsewhere that "all these things happened unto them for enamples: and they are written for our admonition, upon whom the ends of the world are come" (I Corinthians 10:11). To Timothy, Paul said, "All scripture is given by inspiration of God, and is profitable for doctrine, for reproof, for correction, for instruction in righteousness" (II Timothy 3:16). This includes the Hebrew Scriptures. It is necessary, of course, to rightly divide the word of truth (II Timothy 2:15) for it to produce these positive results. Twisting of Scripture results in destruction. (See II Peter 3:16.)

The rest of Paul's answer to the question his letter anticipated was that the Old Testament was written "that we through patience and comfort of the scriptures might have hope" (Romans 15:4). Paul proceeds in this section to quote several passages from the Hebrew Scriptures and to allude to others to demonstrate his point: We learn from and grow in patience and receive comfort—all of which contributes to the establishment of hope—as we study the Hebrew Scriptures.

Contentment Regardless of Circumstances

In his "thank-you" letter to the Philippians to express his gratitude for their repeated financial support (Philippians 4:14-18), Paul wrote, "I have learned, in whatsoever state I am, therewith to be content" (Philippians 4:11). His expression of gratitude to the Philippians was not a veiled attempt to gain their sympathy or to gain more support from them. (See Philippians 4:17.) God had long before taught him how to be content in any situation in life.

The Greek word translated "content" is used only here in the New Testament. It means "self-sufficient." The Stoics, a rigid religious group during the first century, stressed self-denial as opposed to the self-expression promoted by the Epicureans. The Stoics used this word to mean human self-reliance and fortitude, a calm acceptance of life's pressures. The Stoic idea was, "I can make it on my own. I need no one else. By sheer willpower I can do all things."

But Paul's use of the word is quite different. When he says, "I have learned . . . to be content," he means, "By the grace of God I can accept every circumstance—whether negative or positive—in life." (See Philippians 4:12-13.) This was a sufficiency given to Paul by God as a gift, not a self-sufficiency possessed inherently by every human being. Paul's score for successful self-sufficiency apart from the grace of God was as low as that of anyone else. (See Romans 7:15-25.)

During Paul's long ministry, he learned contentment in the midst of extreme circumstances. He wrote, "I know both how to be abased, and I know how to abound: every where and in all things I am instructed both to be full and to be hungry, both to abound and to suffer need" (Philippians 4:12).

These are the same experiences he relates elsewhere: "But in all things approving ourselves as the ministers of God, in much patience, in afflictions, in necessities, in distresses, in stripes, in imprisonments, in tumults, in labours, in watchings, in fastings . . . By honour and dishonour, by evil report and good report: as deceivers, and yet true; as unknown, and yet well known; as dying, and behold, we live; as chastened, and not killed; as sorrowful, yet always rejoicing; as poor, yet making many rich; as having nothing, and yet possessing all things" (II Corinthians 6:4-5, 8-10).

As he reluctantly compared his ministry to that of false teachers, Paul wrote: "Are they ministers of Christ? (I speak as a fool) I am more; in labours more abundant, in stripes above measure, in prisons more frequent, in deaths oft. Of the Jews five times received I forty stripes save one. Thrice I was beaten with rods, once was I stoned; thrice I suffered shipwreck, a night and a day I have been in the deep; in journeyings often, in perils of waters, in perils of robbers, in perils by mine own countrymen, in perils by the heathen, in perils in the city, in perils in the wilderness, in perils in the sea, in perils among false brethren; in weariness and painfulness, in watchings often, in hunger and thirst, in fastings often, in cold and nakedness" (II Corinthians 11:23-27).

But in the midst of these extremely difficult circumstances, Paul was content. He had learned from the Lord how to handle both prosperity and poverty.

Philippians 4:13 is often taken out of its context to mean that believers can do anything they can imagine. Paul wrote, "I can do all things through Christ which strengtheneth me." But the "all things" to which Paul referred are the circumstances he just described in the previous verse. He is not promoting a "positive thinking" approach to Christianity. Nor is he subscribing to the idea of "unlimited human potential." He simply means that Christ gives him the strength to respond in a God-honoring way to every circumstance in which he finds himself, whether it is the positive circumstance of prosperity or the negative circumstance of poverty.

In Philippians 4:14, Paul described the painful circumstances he had experienced as "affliction," and he was grateful that the Philippians shared that experience with him. Paul believed strongly in empathetic ministry. (See Romans 12:15.)

Two Basic Needs

In his first letter to Timothy, Paul wrote: "But godliness with contentment is great gain. For we brought nothing into this world, and it is certain we can carry nothing out. And having food and raiment let us be therewith content" (I Timothy 6:6-8).

It is common in western society to identify three basic needs: food, clothing, and shelter. It may be difficult for us to accept Paul's claim that we should be content with food and clothing alone. But if we remember that he had experienced and accepted an austere lifestyle—including sleeplessness, hunger, thirst, cold and nakedness—it will help us understand his perspective. Since many people, even today, do not have adequate food, if we have food, we should be content. Since many have inadequate clothing, if we have clothing, we should be content.

Whereas contentment coupled with godliness is great gain, or very profitable spiritually, the desire for riches produces all kinds of destructive spiritual consequences: "But they that will be rich fall into temptation and a snare, and into many foolish and hurtful lusts, which drown men in destruction and perdition. For the love of money is the root of all evil: which while some coveted after, they have erred from the faith, and pierced themselves through with many sorrows" (I Timothy 6:9-10).

One of the problems with the Pharisees was that they loved money. (See Luke 16:14.) Paul identified covetousness in the same category as fornication, extortion, and idolatry. (See I Corinthians 5:10-11.) Those who are covetous will not inherit the kingdom of God. (See I Corinthians 6:10; Ephesians 5:5.)

The writer of the letter to the Hebrews admonished his first-century Jewish readers to let their conduct "be without covetousness" and to "be content with such things" as they had (Hebrews 13:5). He supported his statement with Jesus' promise: "I will never leave thee, nor forsake thee" (Hebrews 13:5). In other words, since Jesus is faithful to keep His promise to be with us, we have need of nothing else. Regardless of our material circumstances, we

have an abundant supply in the Spirit. Since this world is not our final home, we should be content with only the basic needs supplied.

Our life in the next world will lack nothing. "They shall hunger no more, neither thirst any more. . . . For the Lamb which is in the midst of the throne shall feed them, and shall lead them unto living fountains of waters: and God shall wipe away all tears from their eyes" (Revelation 7:16-17).

The mature Christian life is distinguished by many character qualities, but none are more significant than patience and contentment. In view of the example of the heroes of Hebrews chapter 11, who by faith demonstrated patience and contentment in the midst of a wide variety of painful circumstances, the writer of Hebrews admonished his readers: "Wherefore seeing we also are compassed about with so great a cloud of witnesses, let us lay aside every weight, and the sin which doth so easily beset us, and let us run with patience the race that is set before us, looking unto Jesus the author and finisher of our faith; who for the joy that was set before him endured the cross, despising the shame, and is set down at the right hand of the throne of God" (Hebrews 12:1-2).

Years ago, a woman approached the late L. D. Segraves with a prayer request. She said, "Please pray for me that God would give me patience." Segraves, an early Oneness Pentecostal minister, placed his hand on her head and began to pray, "Oh, Lord, send this woman tribulation!"

She was horrified. But he explained, "Tribulation worketh patience." (See Romans 5:3.)

There are many who want patience, and they want it now! But Christian character qualities like patience and contentment are shaped only in the fiery trials of life. Those who want these qualities

will find that they are purchased only with the currency of suffering and discomfort.

Test Your Knowledge

1. During what time frame did Job live?
2. Explain the reason for Job's suffering.
3. Discuss the relationship between trials and patience.
4. How do you feel about Paul's claim that we should be content with food and clothing? Why does he not mention shelter?
5. If a person's goal is to be rich, what dangers does he face?

Apply Your Knowledge

For the next seven days, write down every penny you spend, even on impulse purchases and miscellaneous items. At the end of the week, add up your expenditures and determine how much you spent on food. How much on clothing? For what did you spend the rest of the money? Is a significant amount of your finances going to purchase non-essential items? What could you do without with no negative impact on the true quality of your life?

Expand Your Knowledge

Several reports have been written in national and regional magazines and newspapers about the impact of winning a lottery on the lives of the winners. Visit your library and locate one or more of these articles. Share your findings with the class next week. You will discover that, almost without exception, those who quickly obtain riches find the money has a negative and destructive impact on the quality of their lives.